# AN EVENING WITH

# THIS OLD SPOUSE

## By Roger White

### Illustrations by Steve Willgren

Printed in the United States of America

First Printing, 2022

ISBN 978-0-578-38895-3

Written by Roger White

For my Sue. You promised me I'll see you again.
I'm taking it each day until then, my love.

And I really am trying to control the masturbating.

AN EVENING WITH

# THIS OLD SPOUSE

# INTRODUCTION

Long, long ago, when the world was in black and white and married TV couples wore actual pajamas and slept in identical twin beds separated by a night table with a lamp and a pamphlet of instructions on how to survive the nuclear holocaust, there were things called newspapers. Seriously, a bunch of folded, real, ink-nasty paper with words and photos and classified ads for used Buicks—and stories and columns people held in their hands and read. Usually on the toilet. Long stories, too—way longer than the most carefully crafted twitter or meme or insta-thing or whatever.

So, back then, more than a few of these, these "newspapers," ran a column called "This Old Spouse." Penned by a seriously sedentary middle-aged frustrated novelist and husband/father of two, "TOS" was what you would call mini-syndicated in more than a few community newspapers, namely small ones with not much else going on, such as the *Burleson Star, Oak Hill Gazette, Hill Country News, Leander Leader*, and occasionally the back section of the *Bartlesville Auto Trader*.

This column, mostly about daily living with an overfunctioning wife and two precocious daughters, gained quite a following. And when each and every newspaper that faithfully carried "TOS" died a slow and arduous death, the magical column expired with them. And there was a great hue and cry (lots of desperate hueing) from the faithful followers. All seven of them.

So, the column's mastermind, Roger White, a magazine editor and chronic complainer by trade, teamed with his artist pal and mediocre bass player Steve Willgren. If he played bass guitar like he paints, Steve would be Bill Wyman now, but that's another story.

So here, then, are about 53 of the finest examples of a gas-addled man's desperate attempts at humor and immortality—give or take. This is the only comprehensive collection of "This Old Spouse" you'll ever find. Thank God, they said.

Well, there are approximately 117 columns we couldn't fit into this publication. So there may be Volumes II and III eventually. You've been warned. If you're a true glutton, you can find more at oldspouse.wordpress.com. Feel free to Venmo the author whatever you deem appropriate.

# TABLE OF CONTENTS

# WORD TO THE WISE: LISTEN TO THE GANDALF OF GROCERIES

Little by little, year by year, experience by experience, as time has whizzed past my noggin, and my ears have begun to sprout those old-man hairs that somehow generate from deep in the inner canal and hang gray and curly down the earlobe like so many tiny dried-up noodles, it has slowly started to dawn on me how stupid I am.

No, really. I don't mean slackjaw stupid like Junior Samples of "Hee Haw." It's not like I can't balance my checkbook or anything. Well, technically, I can't balance my checkbook, but that's not what I'm talking about. But while we're on this, if you can freely round up and use imaginary numbers in advanced calculus (as I've learned from my high schooler offspring), why can't the credit union let you do the same? Many of my beginning-of-the-month checkbook entries contain the addendum "give or take."

No, I'm referring to life's little lazy assumptions, usually made by husbands, I'm afraid. Here's a good example: the grocery store. For years, when my lovely wife would come home from her semi-weekly food foray with her right eye twitching like a frog leg in a middle school science experiment and using language like my grandpa did in the throes of one of his periodic Battle of the Ardennes flashbacks, I would smile sweetly, offer moral support, and think to myself, "Come on, it's putting milk and eggs and root beer in a shopping cart, get some coping skills, woman."

However, as with the vast majority of my domestic dealings, I found I was oh, so mistaken. I volunteered to venture to the store for family foodstuffs recently—on my own, I must add—and I am here to report that setting foot into the hellish and mystifying jungle that is the local grocery store filled with single-minded shoppers is as terrifying and nerve-crumbling as stalking wild moose with a bow and arrow. In fact, if my family developed a taste for wild moose shanks, I would rather take my chances with the bow and arrow.

I felt smug and confident going in. I had my wife's list; I had my cell phone. How hard could it be? I should have sensed that I was in for trouble when a sage-looking old gentleman, with a white Gandalfian beard and ice-blue eyes, met me going in as he was going out through the sliding doors. He looked at my list, then at me, and he issued a slow, mournful shake of the head. Beware.

The rest was a panicked blur. I will tell you that there is a definite current and flow to grocery shopping,

and if you disturb this current by tarrying too long trying to decipher the difference between cans of diced, crushed, or chopped tomatoes, you will get caught in your own little shopping eddy and spend a dizzying half-hour fighting your way back into the mainstream. I swear I heard "Dueling Banjos" in the distance.

This may be an over-generalization, but, heck, there is always some truth at the heart of generalizations because that's why they're generalizations in the first place. Women are ruthless grocery shoppers. There, I said it. However politically incorrect it may be, I must tell you that in the grocery store you will be run over, sideswiped, given the royal stink-eye, and physically blocked from your desired Chips Ahoy or lean bacon strips by scores of snarling wimmen maneuvering their carts like Richard Petty on prescription amphetamines. My simple theory is that this is their domain, and no man is going to make his hairy presence felt in this, their habitat. I stood quietly behind a diminutive graying little woman for a solid seven minutes while she read every ingredient on a can of artichoke hearts. In any other setting, I would have thought, "what a sweet old lady," but here, she eyed me with a chilling glance, with a look that dared me to utter a sound. I stood frozen, half-smiling until she moved on, and only then was I allowed my turn at the watering hole… I mean, the selection of extra virgin olive oil.

Mind you, I prefaced this column confessing my stupidity, so allow me this: How is it extra virgin olive oil? Virgin, yes. But extra virgin? These olives never even *thought about* going all the way?

Anyway, once I understood the shopping cart pecking order and began to fumble my way around the aisles with a modicum of competence, I found that the list my wife gave me, so simple in the beginning, began to read like hieroglyphics. Everything, and I mean everything, became exponentially more complicated than I ever imagined. For example, apples. The word "apples" was on the list. OK. I hack my way to the fresh fruit section. Sweet mother, I discover, there are 27 varieties, shapes, sizes, and colors of apples, laid out over two aisles of angry, glassy-eyed shoppers. I use my life line. Red delicious, she says. All right, bag 'em. Go, go go. Paddle, boy, paddle.

Same thing happened with the orange juice. Do we need Vitamin C-infused, low pulp, no pulp, extra pulp, mega-pulp, or family style? What in heaven's name is family style orange juice? You pour it in glasses at the dinner table, and each glass of juice begins arguing and grousing about the food? Anyway, I'm at the juice aisle, and in the time it takes me to use the life line again, I incur the wrath of those in the flow behind me. I've created another eddy. The swirling starts again. Help me, Mr. Wizard!

By the time I muddle through the checkout and wander to the exit, I find my hair has become long, white, Gandalfian. I spy a naïve, cocky lad on his way in, his little list in hand. I shake my head at him, slow with just a hint of a wry grin. Beware.

# A DAY AT SIX FLAGS OR WATERBOARDING? HMM, TOUGH ONE

Spring break was winding down and nothing of major importance in the house had been destroyed, the trees in our front yard had remained free of toilet paper, the police had not been called all week to my knowledge, and no one near and dear to me had been injured, died, gotten pregnant, or been hauled to the slammer, so as a reward the wife and I decided to take our lovely daughter and a friend of hers to the nearest Six Flags amusement park. Sweet Jehoshaphat, what a knucklehead idea that was.

First off, it was the last official weekday of spring break. And it is common knowledge that every set of parents in the United States, Canada, Mexico, and some regions of Guatemala clings to the belief that a weekday at a major amusement park will be considerably less crowded than a weekend day. We all truly think that we're the crafty ones and will outsmart all those dimwits who go to the park on a Saturday or Sunday. Hence, everyone piles into the park on that final Friday, making the Six Flags experience not unlike rush hour on a Shanghai subway.

Using this reasoning, I would bet good money that the park is largely abandoned on any given Saturday. But don't quote me on that.

Anyway, we elbowed our way in after almost an hour at the front gate only to find that waiting time for 99.44 percent of the rides was approximately three weeks. Additionally, lines for the bathrooms, conces-

sion stands, souvenir shops, park benches, first-aid stations, oxygen tents, and suicide counselors stretched from west San Antonio to one block from the Alamo. Just about the time we realized this, we body-surfed the crowd to a place called the Flash Pass Booth.

Are you aware of what's transpiring at your friendly amusement park these days? For a fee—and I mean a big, fat fee—you can essentially pay to cut in line. And yes, the line to buy one of these legal cheating devices was down the hall, around the block, and straight on 'til morning. I fully expect within the next year or so that the corporate minds at Six Flags will open another booth at which you may purchase a Flash Pass to cut in line at the Flash Pass Booth. And so on.

Get this, they even have levels of cheating. A Standard Flash Pass is not much better than the common rabble. With a Gold Pass, you move darn close to the front of the line. Platinum—well, you're practically Charlie Sheen here. You can ride twice in a row, kick dirt in the face of one schmuck of your choice still waiting in line, and get your shoes shined while you ride. I predict the eventuality of the Ivanka Trump Pass or some such, wherein you own the damn park and can tell everyone to get lost. This pass, of course, will cost you approximately the Gross National Product of Great Britain.

The whole concept sickened me—almost to the point where we didn't get one.

For a good chunk of our daughter's college fund, we were given the Flash Pass Device: a handheld doodad that looked something like a blood-pressure monitor. In fact, it would be a good idea if this thing could double as one. Mind you, the wife and I passed on the Flash Pass; however, we didn't want our daughter's last official weekday of spring break to be spent standing in one spot in the hot sun for countless hours—which is basically what prisoners of war undergo. So off Lindsey and her friend went, happily cutting in line with the full consent and gratitude of park authorities. A democracy this wasn't.

Now, it's important that I mention here that to ensure that we didn't run off with their precious Flash Pass Device, the smiling Six Flags people held my driver's license for the duration of our visit. Why is this important? Because lo and behold, after a nerve-wracking afternoon working our way through a jam of humanity more bunched together and hostile than a South American soccer match, my wife and I decided it was time for a nice, cold adult beverage. Ahh.

So, then we stood in line for a half-hour at the nice, cold adult beverage stand—only to discover that to purchase a nice, cold adult beverage, you MUST HAVE YOUR I.D. No exceptions. Not even for the Flash Pass doodad, which you leveraged your daughter's future against to purchase in the first place. Plus I haven't been carded since the Nixon Administration! Are you getting the picture of our day at the Disneyland of the Great Southwest?

After a short interim of choice, creative words at various decibel levels, I marched to our car (parked near the Alamo) to retrieve my wife's I.D. Then and only then, after another 45 minutes at yet another libation station, did we get to sit down in the shade (night was falling by now), my wife with a luscious margarita, and me with a $9.50 Budweiser. At this point, price was no object. I would have sold my mother for a beer.

And now the topper. Just as we toasted one another with a long, heavy sigh, our daughter joined us, and in her exuberation, promptly spilled my wife's frozen concoction all over the table. Oh well, there's always Schlitterbahn.

# TAKE HEED, YOUNG MEN, OF CALIFORNIA QUEENS AND LAYERED SHAMS

I used to think life was pretty simple. Learn to ride a bike without killing yourself; dodge the bullies in school; find something you don't mind doing every day for 40 years that keeps peanut butter in the pantry; buy a car that runs; get a home without raccoons.

A simple plan for a simple man—and except for one adolescent NDSE (Near Death Schwinn Experience) and the raccoons, I've been quite successful at following my life's blueprint.

There has been one hitch, however, that has drastically altered my worldview along the way. I got married. (Get it? hitch, married…) Don't get me wrong. As far as female types go, she's a good one; this I've learned in our two-point-five decades together. This I've also learned: Life is complicated. Women know this, and it is their life's mission to teach this to men. Men who have been married as long as I have know this, too.

Don't believe me? I'll give you an example. The bed. Yes, the humble domestic bed. Now, you (you being uneducated men) wouldn't think there would be any measurable amount of pontification or undue stress involved in the purchase and upkeep of one's sleeping spot, would you? Find comfy bed, buy comfy bed, change sheets once a season or so. Ha ha, I say.

Ah, innocent ones, I was once under this misapprehension. When I was a young man, unfettered by responsibilities such as family, home maintenance, regular hygiene, and any income to speak of, my bed was a mattress. I moved often then, and after several third-floor apartment experiences, I viewed such items as box springs, frame and headboard as unnecessary accoutrements. Extremely heavy, unnecessary accoutrements.

I mean, who needs box springs when you have a floor? And except for easy access for nightcrawlers, I found my simple mattress bed to be quite comfortable. I didn't know it at the time, but this was also *tres* fashionable. I discovered years after my bachelorhood that I had been sleeping on a *futon*. Futons became all the rage about the time that hippies grew old, got jobs and realized they had disposable income. The futon wasn't any different from the $5 mattress hippies were sleeping on in college, but by calling it a futon, retailers could jack up the price to, oh, $600. That's called capitalism. The word "futon," by the way, comes from the Japanese. Roughly translated, "futon" means "slob too lazy for real bed."

Anyhow, my inauspicious, perhaps austere sleeping arrangements came to a screeching halt about three minutes after cohabitation (or marriage if this is a family publication). And this was when the bell rang for one of my first lessons in the complexities of life. Shopping for just the right bed, as problematic as that was, was only the beginning. Here are some words actually spoken in our myriad bed-hunting outings (many of these words I had never heard before, seriously): Is that headboard real teak? That's not brown ochre, that's raw umber. (And I thought it was brown, silly me.) Do you prefer negative edge or iron scrolling? I think we have to go with a California Queen.

Although I got an immediate mental image of RuPaul, I was informed that California Queen had something to do with mattress size.

Once we finally found the perfect California teak ochre negative edge bed, I naively presumed that our quest was over. Ha ha, she said. Take out pencil and paper, ye men who are about to marry: There are approximately 3,102 accessories for a bed. I am not joking! Are you ready? There's the:

- Duvet
- Duvet donut
- Duvet cover
- Coverlet
- Dust ruffle
- Mattress topper
- Mattress pad
- Mattress pad cover
- Bed skirt (you want scalloped, pintucked, tailored, or hemstitched?)
- Heated throws
- Sherpa throws
- Pleated shams
- Layered shams
- Bed blouse
- Fitted flats
- Flatted fits
- Matelasse bedspread
- Bamper skiffle
- Skuffler layover
- Berkshire topper
- Tiered voile eyelet perimeter skirting
- Box spring overlay
- Husband (it's a kind of pillow with arms; look it up)
- Toss pillows
- Slouchback
- Sheet smoothers
- And, of course, the oyster-brushed upholstered headboard façade

I didn't even know oysters could brush. And don't get me started about thread count, sister.

Then there's upkeep. Still have your pencils, men? Note: You'll have to change the sheets *at least once a week*, whether they're dirty or not. This includes pillowcases and the odd sock hiding in the covers. Also, the mattress will be flipped and turned every month; I think this is a *feng shui* thing.

I know it sounds grueling, guys, but you'll get the hang of it. Heck, I think I even know the difference between umber and ochre now. One's browner than the other. Now, if we can just do something about the raccoons.

# MR. ALL-DAY SUCKER-HEAD AND YOUR FRIENDLY FIX-IT SHOP

Our little family was tooling along this year, struggling to stay within our monthly budget while juggling life's big-ticket items—you know: braces, home improvement loans, countless teenage daughter items, summer camp fees $x$ number of children$^2$, etc., etc.—when the two most feared words in all of suburbia's lexicon knocked us flat.

Car repair.

Funny thing is, it all started with just a broken brake light. I'm sitting in my wife's car at a stop light, waiting to turn right, when a smiling woman pulls up next to me and says, "Hey, your right rear light is out. Better get it fixed, 'cause the cops will stop you for that."

Instant adrenaline panic overdrive. The cops! Where?

Ever since I was a teenager, having a cop stop me for any reason has always struck fear deep in my heart, even when I was doing absolutely nothing wrong. Readers of a certain age will remember the CSNY lyric: "Like looking in my mirror and seeing a police car!"

So the wife and I promptly hightailed it over to our nearest franchise fix-it shop, thinking that a broken rear light costs, what, five bucks maybe?

Hah. The franchise fix-it shop guys saw us coming a mile away. I should have known. I can't think of any other scenario where I feel so much like a life-sized walking all-day sucker than talking with the mechanic man. I'm thinking I'm not alone on this.

I believe that auto repair types begin sizing you up for the big squeeze the minute you walk in the door.

"Hello, sir, I see you and your wife have a Honda V6."

"Uh, yes."

"Does your model have the actuated re-inverter or self-regulating?"

"What?" Off guard, I blurt, "Actuated, I think. Really, we just need a brake light…"

"Uh oh. Actuated."

(The other guy behind the counter sadly shakes his head at this point. The choreography is keen and well-executed, I must say.)

Still, I play along, because I don't know enough about cars to bluff them, and they know that I don't know. Furthermore, I know that they know I don't know. You know?

Dang, I should have said self-regulating. We're already off on the wrong foot. "Well, it may be self-regulating, I'm not sure."

"No, you said actuated."

"Is that going to be a problem?" I ask.

"Depends. What are you in for?"

"Busted rear light."

"Hmmmm." More head shaking. Some computer clacking, looking in reference manuals.

We left the car with the fix-it shop crew, said three quick Hail Marios to the Great Grease Gods, hoped and prayed for the best, and went about our day. I tried googling "re-inverter," but all I got was something about how to design a death-ray gun. When we got the call that the car was ready, we swallowed our gum, put on our all-day sucker heads, and made our way back to the garage. A different guy behind the counter gave us a bill that was a good 25 percent over the estimate. On the bill was a hefty item—I kid you not—that was labeled "service fee," on top of labor, parts, tax, recycling charges, oil disposal fee, and all the rest.

My wife, always the braver of us, questioned this item, noting that the estimate was much less than the sum before us.

"This is way over what you said," Sue said right out loud, turning all heads in the shop. I cringed. In a western movie, this was one of those moments where the piano player stopped playing and the saloon grew deathly silent. "What is this service charge?"

I expected another stern, condescending talking-to about how variable fluctuations in the world of auto parts derivatives combined with the situation in Libya, hourly swings in crude oil prices, and our particular vehicle's unfortunate re-inverter configuration all coalesced in the time it took to repair our rear brake light to necessitate an additional service charge. But the guy looked at the bill, looked at my wife, and said, "Huh. Don't know what that is. I'll take it off."

Booiiiinnng. That was the sound of my brain leaping out of my skull and bouncing on the floor. How many people, I wondered as I chased my brain across the floor, pay this "service charge" without a second thought?

"By the way, you need new struts. They're bleeding onto your brakes. That's about $600 without tax."

Flush with the confidence instilled by wifey, I took my turn. "Oh, no you don't. I know how you guys operate. Struts. No such thing as struts, I bet."

I got some looks of approval from some of the other guy customers as we walked out of the shop. I think they were looks of approval, anyway. I had a bit of difficulty getting my all-day sucker-head in the car, but we drove away with a bit of salvaged pride. Struts, indeed. What's that noise, hon?

# A BUG BY ANY OTHER NAME WOULD STILL BE A BOMB

It has been brought to my attention recently that I spend much time and space in this forum pining for yesterday. As one of my daughters' buddies put it: "If you love the olden days so much, why don't you marry them?" How does one respond to that? Looking back, I realize I should have said, "Your face!" or something to that effect. Apparently, insults regarding one's visage are the comeback *du jour* among the teen set.

The kid has a point, I guess. In my defense, however, I must emphasize that waxing nostalgic is a cherished rite of passage into geezerdom. Besides, what else am I going to pine for? Tomorrow?

Besides, it has always been this way. Surely, Joe Cro-Magnon sat around the cave in his declining years (which was probably about age 17) grunting on about the salad days of his youth.

"Ah, Neanderthal. Good times. Cave warmer. Women slower."

"Ugh, Dad."

"Don't 'ugh, dad' me!"

Despite my yearning for all things moth-balled, outmoded and sepia-toned, I must confess that the yesterday of my memory likely glosses over events and places and conquests as they really were. The mind has a way of sanding down the warts.

Case in point: my recent Volkswagen adventure. Or as my wife terms it, the Great Bug Fiasco. It's important to note that in the spring of my years, I drove, among other bombs, a VW, cherry red with a killer eight-track stereo and an exhaust system held on with coat hangers. I loved that little car like a boy loves his dog. And this thing smelled like one.

But, man, she was fun—*when she was running*. This is a crucial detail I conveniently fogged over as the years went by.

As I grew older, like so many other family men driving nondescript workaday sedans, I spent much of my adulthood wishing I still had my hippie wheels. Oh, if that old VW could talk, the tales she could tell—and the money I would make because I would have a talking car!

Anyway, one of my benign fantasies of late was searching for just the right Bug to bring back those carefree days. In my spare time, at home, at work, at lunch, at work, at the coffee shop, at work—mainly at work—I would browse web sites like ebay and various car-sales sites. It was purely a personal fiction; I knew I'd never actually go through with it. For one thing, we hadn't the money nor the room for a third car, and swapping the trusty sedan (with all its airbags and terrific gas mileage and dependable brakes and styling like a refrigerator) for a 40-year-old antique wasn't the most prudent move for a middle-income family with two teenage girls and two and a half mortgages. Thing two, I'm about as mechanical as a blind nun—and before all you seeing-impaired women of the cloth start besieging me with treatises on your intimate knowledge of carburetors and intake manifolds, it just sounded good, OK? Thing Three (and this is a big one, so I capitalized the Three), wifey would have absolutely none of it.

With all this in mind, sure enough I found just the right Bug. Oh, was she a sweetie. A 1979 Super Beetle convertible, with new silver paint and a new black cloth top, immaculate interior, working A/C (a VW rarity if there ever was one), and an engine, as far as I could tell. And to top it off, the seller lived in Taylor, just down the road a piece!

Against all odds and adult judgment, I began the beseeching process. Honey, the bug would actually be good on gas. Honey, I could teach the girls how to drive a stick. Honey, the motor on this thing is so simple, even I could fix it. Honey, pleeeeeeease!

Pretty embarrassing, all right. I think she gave in just to shut me up. We met the guy in a Wal-Mart parking lot east of town. I insisted on a thorough inspection and test drive, of course. I drove her once around the Wal-Mart parking lot and said I'd take it. So happy was I, I even named it: Herman the German.

I will say I did have a mechanic give Herman the once-over. He said, and I quote, "It seems to be functioning."

That was good enough for me, so we sealed the deal at my credit union, where Mr. Bug Seller actually shed a few tears. It was then and there I should have remembered my Shakespeare: "The seller doth protest too much, methinks." Hamlet wasn't buying a Volkswagen, but you get the gist.

And you can guess the rest of the story. A week after my proud purchase, Herman began listing severely to the right every time I tapped the brakes. I began to fear the car would keel over on its side if I ever slammed on them too hard. Then one day, on the way home from work, Herman coughed like a cat with a five-pound furball and crapped out right there on the highway. One grim towing bill later, I was told by a mechanic that the engine's fuel intake regulator had compression re-up-take over-valve flatulence or some such. Anyway, he said he fixed it.

He didn't. A week after that, Herman died going to work. I dared to look: the engine was hissing and steaming and spewing black muck like an espresso machine. I didn't know whether to call a mechanic or put a coffee mug under the motor. Mmm. Espresso.

The mechanic got him running again, but the romance was over. I sold Herman to a man from Dallas, and he had that same dreamy look I once had. He had his mechanic look Herman up and down, too, and his grease guy said the same thing mine did. The buyer called me the next week to say the motor konked out on the highway.

What can I tell ya, I said. You want nostalgia, buy a tie-dye t-shirt. It's a hell of a lot cheaper.

# I AM NOT A BEAR

But I play one on TV.

I must warn you from the start that this column is being written while six women sit not 20 feet from me talking about elective surgery and some sort of body treatments that involve the words *exfoliation* and *rehydrating emollients*. Be very quiet.

From the over-the-cubie talk I can't help but pick up, it's a wonder that my big paws can navigate this keyboard with any dexterity at all. Cause I be a may-un. Two syllables. May-un.

…asfkjjjjjjjjjjjjjai67e. Oops. Sorry. Big paws on wrong keys. Burp. Ha ha.

As the token male in an area full of . . . well, you know, females, I have some observations I can no longer keep from spewing forth. So here I spew. When . . . well, you know, females, get together, the conversation inevitably meanders to grousing about males. Either the lack thereof, or the preponderance thereof, or the despicable traits inherent to the species. There are either too many men or not enough men or not the right kind of men or why can't men be women with outdoor plumbing, etc.

From my keen eavesdropping talent, I have compiled the following list of Top 10 Female Gripes About Men. Highly unscientific, I know, but hey, I'm not writing for the *Journal of the American Medical Association* here. Drumroll, please:

**Gripe No. 10: Men don't understand the aesthetic importance of socks.** Even if the male has slowly and painfully learned how to quasi-coordinate clothing and keep such personal hygiene items as fingernails and nostril hair under control, we still don't get it when it comes to socks. We can be as natty as all get out: blue pinstripes, dashing red tie, crisp white shirt, cuff links, stick pin (cue ZZ), BUT: lavender polka-dot hosiery.

*Reason:* They're socks, for crying out loud. Nothing more than underwear for the feet. In fact, did you know that in the alternate universe of Cygnus Y-5, socks are called feetpanties? Should we really care this much about socks? I don't think so.

**Gripe No. 9: If a man had to choose between (A) an evening filled with a free candlelight dinner for two at Fogo de Chao, a moonlit carriage ride through downtown, and unbridled passion by the fireplace at the Presidential Suite of the Driskill Hotel, or (B) catching the fifth game of the Texas Rangers-New York Yankees ACLS, the decision would be a nailbiter.**

*Reason:* What can I say? That competition gene, ya know, handed down through the ages, from having to hunt for food, decipher curveball velocity, and all that. Grunt. This is how our species has stayed alive, ya know. Please remember this when you see us watching sports. It's all about survival.

**Gripe No. 8: Men never ask directions.** Aah, cliche, but true. I once lapped the entire Texas Panhandle several times before giving up and inquiring at a Texaco as to how to gain entrance to Palo Duro Canyon.

*Reason:* We didn't know we were lost. You think Ponce de Leon asked directions? He was an adventurer, damn it. Where's the pioneer spirit? Ooh, look at the gauge, we need gas. And some jerky.

**Gripe No. 7: Men never really listen when women are talking.** Yeah, I attended a good seminar about this. The lady was a top-notch speaker, good-looking, too. Legs! Yow. She had three major points. They were . . . uh.

*Reason:* I'm sorry, what?

**Gripe No. 6: Men just don't get it.**

*Reason:* I'm not sure I understand the complaint. Don't get what? Define *it*.

**Gripe No. 5: Men are simply bears with clothing.** I've heard this often, and since I've never seen a bear with pants on, I can't comment intelligently. So what's wrong with using one's sleeve as a hankie? It's right there, and it's *my sleeve*.

*Reason:* We are simply more casual. Informal. Women can be informal, too, if you work at it. Like washing your hands after going number one. That's actually optional. Crumbs on the couch? Duh. That's why they make the cushions removable. Into the couch cave with ye!

**Gripe No. 4: Men tend to hog the conversation.** I wasn't aware of this problem, were you? Never mind, this guy gave me a great tip about rewiring the DVD player to get free cable, check it out…

*Reason:* This is a business gripe only. If you were a fly on the wall when these men get home, boy oh…

**Gripe No. 3: Men are lazy.** I had a great backup statement here, but I couldn't download it off the computer. And you should see how much there was to key in. Sheesh.

*Reason:* How many times do we have to tell you? We're pacing ourselves. There's a difference. It's a long road, you know.

**Gripe No. 2: Men do half the work for twice the pay.**

*Reason:* Uh, anybody want to field this one? Anyone? Bueller?

And the **No. 1 Gripe About Men according to my highly unscientific over-the-cubie observations of women I know: Men emit sounds loud enough to frighten away livestock.**

*Reason:* Men, men, men, men…It's good to be on a ship with men, men,

# ME AND MY PLACENTA

Viewer warning: For those of you with weak stomachs, strong senses of ick, or those curmudgeonly few who are simply hard of smiling, this column may offend, disgust, bother, or downright nauseate. But it's all true. And in my ever-vigilant quest for truth, justice, and the Appian Way, this seeker of genuine morsels of weird shall not be censored. Unless, of course, my editor nixed this whole idea—in which case you're not reading this. Hmm. So if a columnist writes an article in the forest and nobody reads it, did he really write anything?

So anyway, I read in my local newspaper here that some people, I don't know how many so don't start screaming yet, are keeping their leftover placentas in the freezer for later use. No sir-ree, I did not slip and hit my head on the wet kitchen floor caused by the dog licking at pools of Diet Pepsi, which was spilled by my daughter, who was playing spaghetti games with our emotionally challenged cat at the dinner table. I am not deranged; this statement is true because I read it in the paper. And as we all know, if it's in the newspaper, it must be true.

First off, I have no earthly idea why the adjective "leftover" was stuck in front of the noun "placenta," and I also cannot possibly conceive what sort of "later use" they may be referring to.

So let's read on, shall we? "Our clients are more and more asking to take their placentas home because it's a part of their body, and it's theirs," the owner of a local birthing center said. I would like to insert here that as a card-carrying AARP member, I am unashamed to say that I recently had hemorrhoid surgery, and though it was my body, and those were my parts, I laid absolutely no claim to them when all was said and done. The birthing center woman goes on to say that there are dozens of uses for the placentas, including eating them.

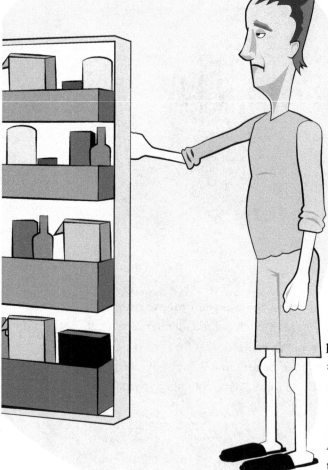

The article notes that although most medical groups do not endorse dining on human placenta, folks who cart their placentas home swear by the nutritional value of this spongy treat—particularly encapsulated placenta, which is, as we are all aware, dried, cured, and crammed into tiny little capsules like so many cold and flu pills.

Sometimes, I get lucky and this column practically writes itself, know what I mean?

Dozens of other uses for the placenta? Let's not go there. Oh, what the heck, I have some more space to fill. Well, for starters, how about an indoor Frisbee? Except good luck ever getting the thing away from the cat once he snags it and high-tails it under the living room sofa. If your neighborhood softball team is thinking of ways of going green, it could make a nifty organic catcher's mitt. All right, that's enough. It's almost lunch time.

Now, as positively grossed out as you may be (and it's perfectly okay if you are because I still have goose pimples and the jimmy-leg as I'm writing this), this sort of thing is nothing new. In fact, folks have been toting home and putting to use all manner of body parts from surgery that were originally destined for that big bio-hazard dump site near Amarillo that nobody wants to talk about. Don't ask. I can't talk about it.

For example, a guy in Scranton, Pennsylvania, finally relented to his wife's wishes and had that delicate operation performed that many boys have done when they are first born. You know. A little off the top, in what the Jewish faith call the practice of Brit milah, or the bris. In keeping with our take-home trend discussed above, this guy now has a nice patio umbrella for his hamster, Rodney.

A housewife in Scottsdale who suffered through years of chronic gallstones now fashions wonderful necklaces and sells them out of her roadside trailer. She uses a strong lacquer finish, so the smell is generally neutral. Yes.

I had a couple more paragraphs here on facial hair and toenails, but my editor is now an off shade of lime.

Well, I warned you at the beginning, didn't I? I gave second, third, and even fourth thoughts about this one, but who am I to put a lamp shade on the truth? Speaking of lamp shades, this one has an odd texture about it. Oh, my—NO!!

# MY ONE AND ONLY NEW YEAR'S RESOLUTION: SILENCE IS GOLDEN

I have one, and only one, resolution that I truly intend to adhere to, as difficult as it may be, for the year 2011. I've made serious resolutions with so many New Year's Days gone by—you know the old standards, losing weight, saving money, drinking less, running more, reading a novel a month, curtailing bodily emissions, actually working at work—all of which have fallen by the wayside within weeks, days, even hours. (Woop, excuse me.)

But this time I mean it.

This solitary promise to myself for 2011, if successfully carried through, could have such significant import and beneficial consequences on not only my way of living and worldview but on those around me that perhaps a groundswell of greater good shall ripple through this land.

I vow, for this year at least, and hopefully on into the days beyond, to refrain from yelling "Free Bird!" at any concert, nightclub show, neighborhood party, school recital, or candidate forum.

Everyone truly hates this guy. Yes, at one time (and one time only) in the distant past, the screaming of "Free Bird!" at public events was original, and even a little funny. I conducted some extensive personal research and discovered the very first use of the "Free Bird!" scream (or FBS, as it's known in this field). The first official utilization of the FBS in an attempt at humor was executed at the Yo Yo Ma concert with

the Orchestra della Scala in Milan, Italy, in the summer of 1980. Near the end of Mr. Ma's (Mr. Yo's?) performance, during a particularly quiet interlude, a young man by the name of Arturo Rossingtono loudly and succinctly requested the Skynyrd anthem from the loge section, at which point he was whisked away by Italian authorities and subsequently spent 13 years in federal detention. Italians take their chamber music quite seriously.

In retrospect, it was an ideal application of the FBS. It was a nice, throaty delivery. Signòr Rossingtono didn't even laugh at his own joke. The juxtaposition of the musical stylings of Ma and Skyrnyd, the classical ambience and considerable risk factor involved, the exquisite timing (combining the acknowledgment that enough grace time had transpired since the Southern rock band's tragic 1977 accident with the fact that the anthem was the most requested concert song since "Stairway"), and, of course, the sublime novelty of it all. It was grand.

Unfortunately for the world, the FBS went from sublime to succotash with one use. And if you think audiences deem the scream a tired prank, consider performers. For one of the most extreme reactions to an audience member using the FBS ploy, go to Youtube and look up Bill Hicks and Free Bird. This marvelous comedian, rest his soul, lost his ever-lovin' mind during a show in Chicago. It was scary, fascinating, and most definitely not meant for younger listeners.

With this painful instance in mind, I must confess that I, too, did spew forth my own rendition of the FBS recently in a public venue. The twelve-string genius Leo Kottke was playing the Paramount Theater in Austin. Mind you, I adore Mr. Kottke. However, the only song of his I really know by name is "Pamela Brown," his only single ever to make the charts. I'd had a couple of fizzy lifting drinks. I was happy and anxious to hear my favorite Leo tune. So, somehow, between songs, while Leo regaled the audience with his tales of wit and insight, it slipped out.

"Pamela Brown!"

My wife hit me in the leg, but it swayed me not in the least. At the next interval, it leapt out again. I couldn't stop it.

"Pamela Brown!"

Leo tuned up some more and then launched into another story. Now, if you've never been to a Kottke concert, understand that listening to his stories is as enrapturing as watching his fingers make like Medusa's hairdo on the frets. Little did I know that this next little talk was aimed at me, however. Leo proceeded to share an experience he had with one particularly stubborn, apparently dimwitted police officer on a rural road. Despite all his protestations and bountiful evidence, Kottke could not convince this country lawman that he did not deserve the citation he was writing.

Leo summed up his tale with a moral: "You can't argue with a moron." He then obligingly played the song I so vociferously requested. I sat there in my seat, all three inches tall, looking up, way up, at my wife, sheepish and silent. Silent I remained for the rest of the show. (I later found out that "Pamela Brown" isn't even a Kottke original. The song was written by Tom T. Hall two years before Leo sang it.)

So, blessedly silent I shall be, for this year at least. If you hear some moron bellowing "Free Bird!" at the next concert, it's not me, buddy.

# BUILDING THE SLOWER MOUSE

I saw my invention on TV the other day, and I had to laugh. Plastic dumbbells, filled with the latest sports drink, were being touted by some company in Norwalk, Connecticut, as the newest workout wonder. You control the amount of weight resistance by the amount of liquid you put in the refillable dumbbells. And if you get thirsty during your routine, simply drink from the weights. Amazing!

Let me take you back a few years. (Imagine your vision becoming wavy as dreamy music carries you to yesteryear…)

I had never actually taken it this far. In the past, either I had never properly incubated the notion or simple next-day logistics torpedoed the whole concept. But this time I'd done it. I had hatched an idea, sketched it, planned its manufacture, and even dreamed of its high-profile marketing. On the tube I could see former Cowboys great Emmitt Smith hawking the Gator-Weights. "I never jog without 'em," would say Emmitt, smiling that Hall of Fame smile and hefting a lime-colored plastic dumbbell. Maybe he'd even autograph them.

A sensational breakthrough that would forever change the aerobic workout paradigm, the Gator-Weights I envisioned as simply two hand-sized hollow plastic dumbbell weights with screw-on tops. When filled with Gatorade (or the athlete's nourishment of choice), the Gator-Weights would provide muscle resistance for the arms in an aerobic workout or simple jog. When the workout's done, the athlete would unscrew the top and replenish those vital fluids. Get some brainy-looking guy with a labcoat and bar charts to attest to Emmitt's claims, and Gator-Weights would swiftly be all the rage. I would have done my part to lower mankind's cholesterol, and I'd be stinking rich.

So there I sat, in the office of Inventor's Friend, some strip-mall cubicle that was supposed to bulldoze a path for my product "straight to the boardrooms of the top corporations worldwide." My mind wandered as I waited my turn. I made a mental list of my favorite vanity plates for the Mercedes. G8RW8. XRSIZ. Or maybe DMBLL.

There were two people ahead of me. Each sat suspiciously eyeing the others, on guard and hunched. The guy next to me, all forehead and cheeks and girth, peered over. He and I were sitting on a black vinyl couch that normally held four. The guy smelled of long-cultivated sweat, and something akin to minted Black Flag Roach Spray.

"What's yours?" the guy wheezed.

"What's my what?" I surreptitiously pressed myself against the far armrest, trying to evade the man's fumes.

"Your invention. What is it?"

I found myself becoming guarded, hunched. I eyeballed the man, then I whispered through the fog,

"What's yours?"

"Movie-roma," he whispered excitedly.

"Movie-ro—?"

"Shshshsh!!"

The other inventor, a woman, looked up. She was guarded, hunched.

My man leaned close and produced from his defoliant-odored overcoat a brass ring, deeply grooved.

"Movie-roma. You know those halos you put on your lamp's light bulbs? Fill 'em with liquid, and they smell like cinnamon, or something stupid like apple-peach?"

I nodded, confidential-like.

"I made the same thing, except I developed aromas you can use for movies." The rotund inventor interpreted my expression as curiosity. "See, it's simple. Say you rent a western. Bring it home, make popcorn, pop in the movie. What's missing?"

"Uh, Movie-roma?"

"Exactly. Take out one of these special aromas I've created, and you have that genuine leather smell. The saddle, the boots, the horses. The movie comes to life."

My silence slowed him not at all. The horses?

"OK. You rent a war movie." The huffing man produced a small case of vials. "This one. Gunpowder.

The stench of war."

"Ah," I said, warily. "Realism. The true multimedia experience."

A representative from Inventor's Friend came from behind a door. He carried a long clipboard, and he smiled, used-car-dealer fashion. He asked for S. Stein. There was no response, and the representative got snippy. "S. Stein, S. Stein. The Petrified Pet." The representative read from a sheet. "Nostalgic throw-back to the Pet Rock. Petrified wood in a cage. Petrified Pet. Hurry, please."

"Oh." The gaunt little woman in a chair against the far wall put down her magazine. She stood, half-raising her hand with a blush. She carried what looked to be a rectangular bird cage fashioned from old coathangers. Inside the primitive cage was a dark chunk of something, presumably petrified wood, nestled in a lump of Spanish moss. Her ticket to the big time.

As the woman followed her Inventor's Friend representative to the recesses of the establishment, I gave serious reconsideration to this whole thing. Dumbbells filled with Gatorade. Hmmm.

I divulged my idea to the Movie-roma Man, with considerably less enthusiasm than I had earlier re-hearsed. His expression was not unlike mine regarding cinematic scents. I could see in his slow nod, "Dumbbells filled with Gatorade. Hmmm."

By the time the next Inventor's Friend representative emerged, I decided to give the Movie-roma Man my place in line. I tossed my home-fashioned dumbbells (Clorox bottles maimed and taped together) in the trash as I left.

I read in the paper several months later that Inventor's Friend was under investigation for fraud. Seems they charged every would-be inventor who stepped in the door, no matter how ridiculous the contraption, a hundred and seventy-five bucks for "application fees and legal research." The place had yet to produce one legitimate invention.

Contemplating my near-brush with fame and fortune, I later scanned the prime-time TV selection. I noted that Nova had a documentary on the marvels of bat guano as crop fertilizer. Wonder what the Movie-roma Man would do with that one?

Gator-Weights, indeed. DMBLL was the choice all right.

(Imagine wavy vision and tinkly piano music as we fast-forward to today…) So now a guy in Norwalk, Connecticut, is making money on my idea. Ah, well. OK, how about this: a flyswatter coated with adhesive, so it picks up squashed bugs as you kill them! Call it the flysucker.

# I'M SOMEBODY NOW!

OK, that does it. Even I have my limits. I received a Call for Contest Entries the other day from the National League of Associations. They're wanting $75 a pop to enter publications or stories in their "internationally recongized competition of professional communicators."

You read it right. Their competition is internationally *recongized*. And I are a professional communicator.

In the (censored) years I've been working at one of Austin's 1,843 nonprofit associations (nine out of ten people in Austin works for Dell, a nonprofit, or the state, according to my non-scientific findings), the number of organizations that send me professional communications contests has tripled. Maybe even fourpled.

Granted, there are legitimate competitions out there in which our association competes in a number of communications categories. And these contests offer not only a shot at awards (and the corresponding banquets with free grub), but also valuable critiques and comparisons with peers in the business. It's fun, it's exciting, and it helps us learn how to do our jobs better. But.

Some of these places that have been sending out the feelers lately, I don't know. The National League of Associations? This begs the question, "Is there an International Association of National Association Leagues?"

On up the chain, you'll have the Interplanetary League of International Association League Guilds. I think.

I get the image of putting two mirrors face to face, I'm not sure why.

There are other such dubious professional organizations. I do believe many of these exist only to engineer such contests, in which they:

(1)  Charge exorbitant entry fees

(2)  Offer genuine photocopied "Certificates of Recongition" (with no substantive critique) to everyone who enters, dead or alive

(3)  Tuck away a tidy sum

Everybody gets an award suitable for framing, and the contest company keeps rolling for another year.

Now, far be it from me to disparage an institution as venerable and respected as Who's Who in American Universities and Colleges, but this here National League of Associations sounds eerily similar to my experience with Who's Who.

I must take you back. Waaay back, to my junior year in college. I won't tell you how far back this is, but let's just say that M*A*S*H was still on prime-time television, Toto was the hot new band, and Bernard L. Madoff Investment Securities LLC was one of the most respected NASDAQ firms in all of Wall Street. By the way, did you know that in order to reach the thirteenth level of a pyramid scheme, every living person in the world would have to be involved? Plus a few dead ones.

So. Ah, yes, I'm in college. I actually got my ducks in order that year, made good grades, got reinstated on my college newspaper staff (because they could not prove that I was driving or that any of that stuff was mine), and came in third playing drums in a campus talent show. By the end of that semester, I got an official-looking letter in the mail saying I qualified for Who's Who in American Universities and Colleges. Hot damn! Third place at the talent show probably clinched it.

Well, my folks got the same letter, and, sure enough, they ordered that year's official *Who's Who in American Universities and Colleges Compendium of Honorees*. Oh, brother. It was a book as fat as the *American Heritage Dictionary* (unabridged), containing no less than 25,000 names and bios in tiny, little print. My mom still hasn't found my name.

Remember the movie "The Jerk"? Steve Martin? Yeah, that scene. "The new phone books are here! The new phone books are here! I'm somebody now!"

Here's another good example. Have you seen ads in the backs of magazines and newspapers for the National Poetry Contest? There is no entry fee, but (big but here) each contestant gets a chance at not only prize money, but—staccato breath here—publication in the prestigious *National Anthology of American Poems and Prose*!

Aha. My gut tells me that although prize money is frugally doled (if at all), every would-be Walt Whitman gets published. The money-maker here is that 43,011 frustrated poets purchase this lovely leather-caressed *Anthology of the American Spirit of Gullbility* for only $69.99 to see their work hardbound. Voila! They're published poets!

It's a sure tipoff that a scam is brewing when one of the anthology's featured poems begins thusly:

"There once was a young man from Nantucket . . ."

But, hey, I got a neat certificate of recongition.

# ROLLING THE JARGON DICE

Understand as I launch into this column that I work for an education association. And I have worked for this education association for a long, long time. In my long, long time with this education association, I've learned many things. However, I think the main thing I've learned is that people in the education world speak a language that is very different from normal humans. (Now, let me tell you that I'm talking management types here—you know, campus administrators and on up. If actual teachers talked this way, all of America's children would be wandering about, zombie-like and unblinking. Like Joaquin Phoenix.)

Anyway, in my tenure here, I have come not only to understand education jargon, I have learned to embrace it. Therefore, I founded EJUCIMUSE.

And here at the EJUCIMUSE Headquarters (EJUCIMUSE being an acronym for Education Jargon Use Cause It Makes Us Sound Elite, of course), in our ever-vigilant attempts to utilize jargon, gibberish, and edu-speak whenever possible, we are proud to announce the creation of the MANURE Generator.

MANURE (Mechanism to Advance New Understanding for Renewal in Education) is the brainchild of Jerry Taylor, educational technology director for Arcadia Middle School in Greece, New York. Taylor unveiled the MANURE Generator not long ago in the National School Boards Association's *School Board News* newsletter, and it has been getting rave reviews . . . I mean, its outcomes-based approach dynamic has received initial focus-group consensus.

Here's how MANURE was formed: According to Taylor, throughout his 30-year career as a teacher (also known in some circles as transitive knowledge facilitator), noticed that many teach–, sorry, many transitive knowledge facilitators and knowledge transfer management personnel (administrators) sometimes fall behind in their utilization of proper edu-speak. So Taylor made MANURE. This fascinating device not only can keep edu-speak proponents up-to-the-minute, it makes a great party game and a nice dessert topping.

Now here's how MANURE works: If you are ever caught at a meeting, focus group, performance evaluation, or happy hour shop talk without the latest edu-speak term or phrase, simply whip out your pocket-sized MANURE Generator and a pair of dice. You'll soon be spouting the most eloquent of nonsensical jargon.

The MANURE Generator consists of three columns of words. These could be called Column A, B, and C. But for our purposes, we'll call them Initializing Column I(a), Activating Column II(b), and Terminus Column III(c).

And here they are:

| Initializing Column | Activating Column | Terminus Column |
| --- | --- | --- |
| 2. Integrated | Behavioral | Strategies |
| 3. Individualized | Relevant | Methodology |
| 4. Criteria | Assessment | Cooperative |
| 5. Flexible | Prescriptive | Analysis |
| 6. Authentic | Perceptual | Learning |
| 7. Facilitated | Interaction | Functions |
| 8. Responsive | Modular | Objectives |
| 9. Alternative | Diagnostic | Concept |
| 10. Performance | Structured | Recovery |
| 11. Cognitive | Situational | Management |
| 12. Systemic | Evaluative | Reform |

Simply roll the dice (otherwise known as the MANURE Generator Activation Modules) to select a word from the Initializing Column, a word from the Activating Column, and one from the Terminus Column. Do you want fried or steamed rice with that? Note that since you can't roll a 1, the columns start at No. 2, Einstein. Voila! It's that easy.

You'll have your colleagues wanting desperately to know more about Facilitated Situational Objectives with quick rolls of 7, 11, and 8. Land on 11, 2, 6 and you have created the Cognitive Behavorial Learning school of thought.

The great thing is, you don't necessarily have to work in the education world to avail yourself of this sensational tool. A tinker here and there to the columns as necessary can produce a powerful jargon generator for any business. In other words, put your hands in the MANURE, work it around a bit, and you can easily shape it to your liking.

Then I believe you should wash your hands.

I must say that we here at EJUCIMUSE have been so impressed by Taylor's MANURE that we unanimously voted him Edu-Speak Vociferator of the Biennium. We got a plaque for him and everything, but Taylor couldn't make the awards ceremony. He was giving a lecture in Washington, D.C., on Alternative Diagnostic Recovery.

# TIRED OF YOUR UNWANTED GOLD? AND OTHER STUFF

I can't make up stuff to write about that is any sillier than real life. And if I did make it up, you wouldn't read it because you would say, "Oh, he's just making that stuff up, and it's silly." But you do read this stuff because you know I'm not making it up because I wouldn't be silly enough to make this stuff up. This is *real stuff*, and that's why it's funny. And isn't "stuff" a funny word? Say it out loud. Stuff. See? Kind of like rhubarb.

Here's an example of the stuff I'm talking about—and I promise not to stay "stuff" any further in this venue. Have you seen the TV commercial in which the benevolent, dulcimer-toned gentleman asks if you are tired of your unwanted gold? I kid you not, this is a genuine television commercial. And when I saw this one, it was one of those coffee-spewing moments. Got Folgers' all over the dog.

In the ad, this poor woman is at her cluttered and unkempt jewelry box, surrounded by junky mounds of tasteless gold bracelets, rings, necklaces, and tacky Krugerrand coins. The horror. But, thanks to Gold-Away (name changed to protect the perpetrators), she can send all that nasty gold (in an envelope, mind you!) off to Connecticut – why is it always either Connecticut or New Jersey? – and even get some money in return!

Yes, not only is this beleaguered gal now able to shed those unsightly precious metals, she gets paid for it. Something along the lines of $5.00 per pound!

The only thing more stunning to me than the premise of this commercial is the fact that *it has been running for months*—which means it must be working! Try as I might, I just can't imagine the scenario. But here goes:

"Damn it, hon, if I trip over any of this gold bullion one more time, I'm gonna fling the cat! Why do we have all this old, klunky gold lying around?"

"Now, Jethro, don't get yer antlers all twisted. We can send it off to Gold-Away in these here special envelopes, and they'll take care of it for us."

"Well, thank heaven for Gold-Away. I think I broke my big toe."

The same principle (that principle being, of course, taking as much advantage of the feeble-minded as is corporately possible) applies to just about anything and everything produced by a certain mint named after the bespectacled philosopher-statesman who got struck by lightning whilst flying a kite. I won't mention the mint by name for fear of legal action, but let's just call it the "Benjamin Mint."

Have you seen what these guys are offering? Get this, you can purchase, for example, the entire 11-coin Sacagawea 2000-2010 Dollar Coin Collection—if you act now!—for only $99.00. The mint fails to mention that each of these "rare" coins is worth precisely one dollar each, and they're all in circulation. So if you go to the laundromat or get change from Starbucks often enough, you'll find them. For, oh, about eleven bucks. Total.

Ah, but this particular Sacagawea set comes in a handsomely crafted box with crushed velvet and shellac and all that, the Benjamin people will argue. My answer, Hobby Lobby or Michael's, ten bucks.

It gets worse. I shall now read from the brochure: "These coins are made from pure copper with a manganese brass outer clad!" What do they think the Sacagaweas on the street are made of—tomato aspic?

Again, this is real life. Why would I lie?

It is the apparent success of ads and commercials such as these that dims my hopes for this mighty nation—that and the verbal spewings of a certain politicos who shall remain nameless. And more importantly, it makes me almost want to stop watching TV. Almost. Instead, I keep one of those nifty foam bricks within arm's reach of the recliner. A well-aimed toss of this baby right into the kisser of the benevolent, dulcimer-toned Gold-Away man does wonders for the blood pressure.

I was lucky to get my foam brick, too. There was a limited supply, the TV guy said, and I called just within the 20-minute window to get the insider's deal—two bricks for the price of one, plus shipping and handling. Sweet!

# YOU KNOW WHY TAXES ARE SO HARD? ALIENS.

Take off the tin-foil hats, stop stockpiling Clark bars and juice, cancel the ham radio lessons. I know for a fact that aliens will never take over the world, at least not by subterfuge. You've seen the movies. You know, like "Invasion of the Body Snatchers," where devious Martian misanthropes spring from overgrown green pea pods and disguise themselves as everyday people, except that they never can get the recipe for human expression down quite right. They always end up with all the charm, personality and emotional sincerity of a Bjorn Borg or a Keanu Reeves. Why is this man an actor, by the way? Name me one movie in which Keanu Reeves shows one iota of any kind of acting skill. He's only up there on the big screen because he's cute and has nice hair. It isn't the American way to put people in positions of power merely because they're cute and have nice hair, is it? Um, never mind.

In real life, lack of sincere emotion wouldn't be the giveaway for the alien hordes, though. Before it ever came down to a clash between our puny weapons and their ultra-cool technology, before they ever began shedding their human cloaks and herding us like Nike-shod cattle into sleek, gray rooms for horrifying experimentation (why are aliens so obsessed with probing our backsides, anyway? the pervs), the aliens would be exposed because of one aspect of the human condition that we all take for granted living on planet earth. And no, I'm not talking about germs. You think aliens don't know about germs? Please. Look at them, they're crawling with germs—they even look like germs, for crying out loud.

No, what will trip up our outer-space adversaries in their quest for domination of our cozy little blue marble will be the tax code. No living being, even those with brains the size of washing machines, can sit at a table with a tax booklet, paper, and pencil and rationally decipher the 1040 form. I tried to fill out our taxes last weekend, and after five hours of earnest weeping, two forests of crumpled papers, eight cups of jet-black coffee, six screaming tirades, and one rather unsettling episode of giggling, I gave up because one of my ears started bleeding.

I truly believe that the people who concoct the questions on the 1040 form are sadistic former psychology majors. Remember when you were in college, and you volunteered for that study where the psychology major puts you alone in a room (with the two-way mirror) and tells you to jump up and down on one foot while tossing a tennis ball in the air until he comes back to tell you to stop? The study is not about manual dexterity; it's about how gullible you are. (I was the guy who kept jumping and tossing. I don't like to make waves. I was afraid of some sort of punishment if I stopped.)

Anyway, it's the same principle with the tax forms. I mean, come on:

**48.** Go back to line 7. Now, if the total of Line 7 and Line 9 equals the square root of your 1974 tax return's weight in metric grams, then fold Form 299A (see instructions) at right angles and multiply the hypotenuse of the resulting triangle by the total exhaust emissions from your spouse's vehicle during the previous year's cloudiest week (not counting June and September in Arizona and/or Cincinnati). If not, then enter zero unless you are claiming the $2,000 patriot provision as found in Form S81 Subform 32xL (see the man in the coat). Now, …

If you look really hard, you'll notice some squiggly lines on some of these questions on the 1040 form. You know what that's from? The IRS guys laughing so hard that they fell over on the copying machine, which smudged the form. You know and I know it doesn't have to be this hard.

Then again, maybe it does. This is what keeps us safe from the aliens. Any time an alien advance force takes human shape and tries to blend in with us, they are always outed, without fail, when their heads explode as they attempt to do their taxes.

God bless America.

# HERE'S TO THE ROYAL COUPLE! CLINK. HIC.

I simply cannot tell you what the royal wedding between Prince William and Kate Middleton meant to me. No, wait, actually I can. In four words.

Toad in the hole.

As most regular guys will attest, all the pomp and majesty and gowns and uniforms and beefeaters and archbishops and romance and cleavage do very little for us. Well, maybe the cleavage. Otherwise, to the average American Joe Blow—who comprises 92 percent of the U.S. male population (97.7 percent of Oak Hill men, huzzah!)—watching coverage of the royal hitching could be likened to sitting through a televised reading of the Congressional roll call.

Ho. Period. Hum. Exclamation mark.

Highlights of the actual ceremony for us Joes?

- Posh Spice (aka Mrs. David Beckham, hubbah hubbah)
- Pippa Middleton (Kate's sister, who followed the bride around carrying the dress's caboose—again with the hubbahs)

- That gorgeous droptop Aston Martin the royal couple tooled down the road in. Now we're talking. I did some research and found that this awesome ride, which Wills borrowed from his dad, is a 1969 DB6 Mk2. This car, sweeter than any bridal gown the House of Steve McQueen or whatever could produce, is fueled by a four-liter double-overhead cam six-cylinder powerplant, churning out over 280 horsepower at 5,500 rpm. Not a V6, mind you. No, this is an old-world inline six. Righteous. William cruised off to his mom's palace using a five-speed manual transmission, by the way. So there was no playing handsies in the car; he was working a stick. How 'bout that for wedding reporting, guys?

So, anyway, about the toad in the hole. After watching the newly minted royal spouses speed away in a car likely worth more than double my lifetime earnings, I figured that was it for me—no more happy royal nuptial news, please.

Then I heard National Public Radio's coverage of various "wedding watching" parties across the country. Apparently, many, many ladies throughout our fair land got up at three a.m. to bear personal witness to all the glitter and gowns and unicorns and such. But they didn't simply crawl out of bed and turn on the tube. No, they gathered in brightly colored klatches, baked up all sorts of British fare, mixed up champagne and orange juice, champagne and cranberry juice, champagne and prune juice, champagne and more champagne, and made genuine little festivals out of the whole affair.

I'm thinking the female work force in the U.S. and U.K. was pretty sparse later that day.

Listening to the women carry on at these shindigs in NPR's story made me a tad envious, I must admit—and hungry. Some of the properly British dishes served at these gala gatherings included chocolate scones, bubble and squeak, toad in the hole, egg in a basket, fruit bismarcks, smoked haddock, truffles, rashers, black pudding, and, of course, fish 'n' chips with Guinness.

First off, bubble and squeak. Sounds like a bathtub cleaner, I know, but it's really quite yummy. You take leftover roast and veggies, throw in some potatoes, cabbage, carrots, peas, and other odds and ends and fry it up in a pan. To be perfectly cheerio, you serve it with pickles.

Toad in a hole? Sausages in pudding batter, slathered in onion gravy, and baked like a casserole. Never tried it myself, but oh, it sounded good. The Pavlovian dog in me heard the bell quite plainly.

What else? Ah, egg in a basket. Remember the movie Moonstruck? When Olympia Dukakis was frying up an egg in a piece of toast? Again, ding! Rashers—basically, that's British bacon. Fruit bismarck? Easy, that's essentially a big ol' mixed fruit pie gobbed with powdered sugar and whipped cream. The rest of the royal rations you can probably guess.

And, of course, the whole lot is washed down with ample servings of champagne with (insert fruit here) juice and/or beer stout enough to walk on.

As I listened to the recipes pile up in this story, I realized the common denominator was booze of one sort or another. Aha! There, I determined, lied the ulterior motive for many of these stately soirées. These ladies only claimed interest in the House of Windsor's succession rituals just to catch a buzz. Sheesh, some people.

Well, it's all over and done with, anyway. Hand me a Miller Lite, will ya? The game is on in a few.

# 'SCUSE ME WHILE I KISS THIS GUY

For this installment to make any sense to you, my fellow life travelers, it will behoove you to be of a certain age range—namely, somewhat old to pretty darn old. It will also be of great benefit to your reading comprehension and pleasure if you are listeners of a particular genre of music—i.e., rock and roll that also ranges from somewhat old to pretty darn old.

Let's put the bandwidth at somewhere grayer than The Cars but not so geriatric as Jerry Lee Lewis. Give or take. So if you don't currently fit these parameters, I will wait to write the rest of this column until you comply. You have 20 minutes.

Oh, forget it. I got stuff to do. Please continue.

You see, it occurred to me the other day, as I tried with scant success to decipher the words to one of the endless string of hippity-hop rapster tunes my daughters devote their entire afternoons to (see previous column entitled…well, heck, see all previous columns), what wondrous adaptive mechanisms our brains are. If we can't make out the lyrics to a song we listen to over and over (sometimes under duress), our minds create lyrics for us—and even a backstory to go with those faux lyrics—so we can make sense of what we're hearing and thus not go entirely insane.

Specifically, I was driving home from a genuinely miserable day at the cube. The
radio was still in daughter mode, so
when I turned it on, Katy Perry
was asking plaintively, "Baby, are
you tired of work?" You know
it, sister, I replied. Understand that I recognized the
singer only because I have
been taken to task several
times for not knowing who
Katy Perry is or realizing her
great significance to Western
civilization. My daughters truly
believe it is my life's goal to embarrass
the bejeezus out of both of them.

So anyway, I got home and relayed with a smid-
gen of pride to my girls how I related to Ms. Perry's
song. I got the exaggerated eye roll and the pitiful head
shake, in unison. "Dad, you are such a goober. She's saying,
'Baby, you're a firework.'"

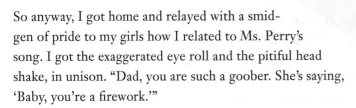

Oh. Well. It was then I hopped into my lemon-yellow time
machine and found myself back in my senior year in high
school, working at that tiny self-serve gas station, stacking cans of Pennzoil in the back. It was 1976, and
the cheap box of a radio in the next room was playing the new song by The Eagles, hot off the presses.
What follows I must say in my defense transpired mainly because I couldn't hear that darn radio very well.
Did I mention the radio was cheap, and small? Anyway:

Catchy tune, I thought as I strained to listen, and what a unique way to give vent to how things can get so
messed up at times:

> "Flies in the Vaseline,
>
> Surely make you lose your mind,
>
> Flies in the Vaseline, uh huh…"

I could identify with that. I asked my friend the next day if he'd heard the song. "Neat," I said, "because
it's true, ya know. Sometimes it feels like there's just a bunch of flies in your Vaseline. Everything going all
wrong."

My buddy's face morphed from utter confusion to complete hysterics when it dawned on him that I was talking about "Life in the Fast Lane."

Just so you'll know I'm not the only goober in the family (and so I can shine the warm lights of shame on my wife, as well), when I divulged my dark secret some years ago to my lovely spouse, Sue, she laid on me a beauty of a "lyric lapse" of her own. Now, here's where you may look at me like a medicated cow if you haven't heard the song.

My dear Sue actually thought that in the song "Peace of Mind" by Boston, where the chorus goes thusly:

> "I understand about indecision,
>
> But I don't care if I get behind…"

…that it went like this:

> "I understand about indecision,
>
> But I'm not scared of the FBI…"

I thought for a while there that she was just saying this to ease my discomfort, but no, you can't make this stuff up. We surely all have our own versions of tunes, the most classic being, of course, "'Scuse me while I kiss this guy…" I bet Jimi never knew how many people through the years would be pondering his lifestyle choices because of that one line. And, yes, CCR will always and forever be accused of some sort of scatological preoccupation for directing us to the "bathroom on the right."

There are dozens, probably hundreds of others. There are even books and web sites devoted to this phenomenon. But you can't really worry about it. It happens to everyone, I guess. You have to just let the water run off your back, like Van Morrison says in "Brown-Eyed Girl":

> "Hey, wet amigo!
>
> Dazed when the rains came…"

# WHATEVER HAPPENED TO DAIRY QUEENS AND SNAKE FARMS?

A quick gander at the calendar on the old wall shows that it's actually summer now, which means it's just about vacation time again. Which means it's time for Dad to take a second and third job. I figure that a few weeks of mowing lawns and cold-calling potential investors for the Happy Shores Time-Share Villas in Enid, Oklahoma (in addition to my regular 40-hour editing gig), will put just enough in the family coffers for a week of, uh, "summer fun."

Call me old, call me out of touch, call me cranky, but the family vacation just isn't what it used to be. And I'm not just talking about the cost—although I'm mainly talking about the cost. Remember when your parents would gas up the station wagon, pile you and your siblings and the dog and just about anything else that would fit into the back, and aim the car at the nearest national park? And the trip always started at 4 a.m. No matter the destination, you were rousted from bed, still slobbering and sleepwalking, hustled into the car in the black of night, and whisked off like a fresh cult recruit. That was the vacation. No questions asked, no negotiations, no whining.

And you were grateful for any and all unscheduled pit stops along the way. For you readers who happened to be boys back then, you'll recall that if your dad was far enough behind schedule en route to the Petrified Forest, your pit stop was a coke bottle. Nuff said. The wheels had to keep rolling.

Thing of it is, as much as we old-timers enjoy grousing about just how spartan and militarily executed the vacations of our youth were, we actually look back on them fondly. Sort of. You must admit, the rules of the road were different. If you could fit in the rear window deck, and who couldn't back then, you had

a vista view for the entire ride to Carlsbad Caverns. The back floorboard, with the massive transmission lump in the middle, served as a two-bedroom suite. You could always tell quite easily what other vehicles were in vacation mode on the highway by all the arms and legs and feet and various other body parts hanging out the windows.

Meals and entertainment consisted of Dairy Queens and Snake Farms. And to my 9-year-old sensibilities, visiting the roadside Snake Farm was on par with the Taj Mahal, the Statue of Liberty, or any other great wonder of man or Mother Nature. In fact, somebody should write a country song about old-time vacations—and call it "Dairy Queens & Snake Farms." I'm not much of a country fan—I'm more of an old rock and roller—but I would buy this record. (It wouldn't be available on iTunes, by the way, only on 45-rpm records. Nyah.)

And lodging was simple back then. Once we hit our destination, the nearest motor lodge that didn't have a red "No" winking in front of the neon "Vacancy" sign became vacation central. The TV menu was whatever local stations the motel set's rabbit ears could pick up, and in-room recreation involved either Nerf basketball with a small trash can or clandestine trampoline wars between beds while the parents were out of the room getting ice.

Today? Well, our kids have been on more airplanes than I ever saw as a youngster. Island resorts, all-inclusive fantasy-land amusement parks, and fancy fondue restaurants cater to every whim. The latest movies and 3-D videos are in the hotel room and on the iPad, which means constant state-of-the-art entertainment anytime all the time. "Hey, look out the window, kids! Get a load of that sunset!" "Yeah, sure, Dad, whatevs." Clickety clackety click click.

I have truly come to hate that texting sound.

It's our own fault, really. There is peer pressure, of course, especially when you hear your kid's friend casually mention how boring Italy was this year. But it is time to make a stand. Who's with me? We have to draw a line in the sand—and I don't mean the alabaster sand of the all-inclusive Atlantis Paradise Island in the Bahamas. If we raise a crop of jaded, spoiled teens, you know what they'll become? That's right! Kardashians! Gads.

I mean it. This year, we're piling everybody into the car, throwing the texting, beeping, streaming pod-things out the window, and heading nonstop to the great outdoors. Isn't that right, hun? Hun?

"What's that, dear?" Clickety clackety click click.

Hmm.

"Hello, this is Roger with Happy Shores Time-Share Villas of Enid, Oklahoma. Have I got a deal for you. . ."

# IT'S BUMPER TO BUMPER ON MY STREET OF CONSCIOUSNESS

*Note to self: For drive home from work, play Burt Bacharach CD, not Black Sabbath. Remember that vein in your forehead.*

I've been inching my way along these city roads to and from the old salt mine for about 30 years now. Thirty. Long. Years. I wonder what people who really do work in salt mines call their place of employ? The old pit o' hell? And what about the folks under contract to old pits o' hell? The old eternal damnation parlor, perhaps? Hmm. Darn rabbit holes.

But traffic's only gotten worse, hasn't it? You know it's bad when you can look down from your vehicle and recognize the same cigarette butt and discarded lottery ticket at that same spot in the road you were at yesterday. Man, one more scratched-off cherry, and the guy would've been on easy street. Ah, well. Probably bumper to bumper there, too. Why does everything get worse? Even for me, a professed curmudge, pining for the good old days can be a tad depressing at times. Surely there's light somewhere at the end of this tunnel we call today's living. I know, I know, that light may be an oncoming train. But if life keeps going this way, will we be three deep in cars by the time our grandkids are geezers? Will it all really be a bleak Blade Runner landscape by the time Justin Bieber checks into the Hair Club for Men?

Nevertheless, the whole workaday driving ritual is unique theater, isn't it? And it's not just the fact that normal, mild-mannered people morph into heartless, seething jerks once they slip into their shiny metal boxes. It's the whole dance, the instant alliances, the one-minute wars, the hand gestures, the traffic-light trysts, the old blind-spot head bobs ("I'm sorry! I didn't see you!"), the split-second decisions to be either magnanimous or dictatorial. "You may enter. You, I do not care for. You will wait."

It's all so melodramatic, Wagnerian even.

Traffic is its own world, really. For me, there are three main components of living: home life, work life, and traffic life. Well, and in-law visit life (help me, God), so four. Oh, and weekend TV sports life, which sort of cancels out in-law visit life, so that makes five, unless you rule that they canceled each other out, in which case we're back to three. That's up to you. But my point is, the daily commute is such a pancreas-twisting hassle that you must emotionally gird yourself to face it every working morning and eve. I for one think we should be compensated for daily accepting the awful challenge. Yes! I say if our places of business won't pony up, then we demand that the state give us our due for having to get up, get clean, and battle each other tooth and nail and fender every day just to eke out a living.

But I will tell you this, fellow commuters. Try to have patience with the 21-year-old male driver in his uber-tuned Subaru XYZ-7 or whatever with the ridiculous silver tailpipe as big as a pregnant alligator and that stupid wing on the trunk that looks like something off of Mario Andretti's Indy racer. The 21-year-old male driver cannot be blamed for thinking he won't be late for work if he stays one-point-one millimeters from your back bumper screaming and snarling at you to die all the way from one end of town to the other. Because he is overflowing with hormones. Yes, I know, we all have hormones—but they're not like his hormones. Medical researchers have actually studied 21-year-old male hormones under a microscope, and they found that all the tiny little hormones are all riding each other's tiny little bumpers screaming and cursing all up and down the bloodstream. So it can't be helped.

Just like old lady drivers can't be blamed for doing the old lady thing. I know, believe me. I used to be a 21-year-old male driver, and now I'm pretty much an old lady driver. I still use the men's restroom, but, yeah, for all intents and purposes, I'm an OLD (Old Lady Driver) now.

So get off my tail, sonny.

# OF VARIABLE RATE CRAYONS AND ENDOSCOPIC CLAMBAKES

I'm on some interesting meds now. Let's see if you can tell:

We're pretty sure my paternal grandmother had six toes on each foot, just so you'll know. I never saw my grandmother's feet; in fact, she died before I was born, but I heard the stories. She could swim like crazy. They called her Ol' Paddlefoot.

It was good to get that out of the way. I feel better, don't you? But back to Facebook, I don't understand why anyone wants to poke, or be poked by, another person on this here Facenook network. There should be buttons other than "poke," like thump, prod, sniff, eviscerate, wedgie, scoot, bump, smack, query, shine, tease, smear, annihilate, fondle, inebriate, push, fluff, excoriate, grope, lick, claw, hack, weatherproof, annoy, rub, polish, whittle, and, of course, probe. And perhaps shower.

Meanwhile, here are some words that I dare say have never been this close together before:

- Annuitized shoehorn
- Marsupial term life plan
- Heartwarming guillotine
- Variable rate crayon

- Chocolate-covered plutonium

- Endoscopic clambake

- Semi-automatic pudding

Now to cats. I was on the back porch with my cat, Max, the other day, and I noticed this bizarre tic he has. Max is a gorgeous tortoise-shell tabby, gray and black swirled with a burl undertone. He looks like a raccoon without the bandit eyes, and he pets like a chinchilla. He's very luxurious, and he knows it. He preens a lot. He's overweight but quite athletic, as all cats are. Whenever Max spies potential prey, be it a swooping silver hawk, a chittering squirrel, or a wind-blown piece of yard lint, he starts issuing these short, choppy meow bits, bouncing his jaw up and down like he's having a conniption fit. (Please note that some dictionaries make a clear distinction between a conniption fit and a hissy fit. A conniption fit involves many more overt physical movements and gyrations. Apparently, a hissy fit entails merely verbal gymnastics.)

Max maintains this behavior until he either starts wiggling his butt to go into attack mode or gets bored and falls asleep. Usually, he chooses sleep. Sometimes he attacks. Other times, he falls asleep in the midst of an attack. It's all rather embarrassing. But he's our cat, and we love him. I mention Max because it is he who basically runs the household. Max determines whether Ralph, our long-haired daschund, may pass him in the hallway without assault. It is Max who wakes my wife and me up in the morning by kneading our respective chests until we either throw him to the wall or get up and greet the day, and it's almost always the latter. It is Max who informs each family member when it is mealtime, and it is Max who keeps the family on our collective toes by zipping at light speed out any door opened at any place in the house at any time. How he does this I do not know. I think Max has a GPS map of our house and all its access points linked to his kitty box or something. And I have heard electronic-sounding beeps and boops coming from his box—even when I know Max isn't in there. Get this, Max can be at the far end of the house, snoozing away with his back feet in the air, but as soon as I crack the garage door just the tiniest bit—PHOOOM!! He's gone.

The good thing about Max is that he doesn't roam. He just stands there in the yard, eating grass blades and taking the occasional dirt bath. I think he's just proving a point. "Yep, I can blow this popsicle stand any ol' time I want. Mm hm."

For some reason, Max stalks our youngest daughter, Jamie, like she's wild jungle prey. With the rest of us, he meows and purrs and does the usual cat protocol, but every time he spies our young one he flashes to Arnold Schwarzenegger in that movie with the invisible alien hunter dude. "Get the choppah. RR-ROOWWRRR." Max and Jamie fight like, well, like cats. I think Max is under the impression that Jamie is another cat. I guess I can see that. I do keep trying to tell Max that Jamie is a human being, but he always looks at me like I'm a used car salesman or something.

OK, why don't we end this installment with more words that have never shared a sleeping bag:

• Terrycloth opinion

• Inspirational vivisection

• Polyunsaturated mortgage

• Peppermint amputation

• Lightly salted lawsuit

# I PLAYED DRUMS FOR FRANK ZAPPA—DIDN'T I?

One of the few nice things about growing old is that the more ancient you become, the less you can be blamed for how quirky and oddly selective your memory is. We boomers (aka flower children, hippies, yippies, Owsley's owls, hepcats, heads, groks, hipsters, space cadets, longhairs, psychedelic cosmonauts, merry pranksters, etc.) are also able to bask in the added bonus of being able to point the flying fickle finger of forgetfulness at all that, um, consciousness-expanding experimentation of our salad days as yet another source of our cumulus-dotted craniums. Or is that cranii? Craniundum. Whatever.

As one sage and far out philosopher once pined: "If you remember the '60s, then you weren't there." At times, I regard this statement as the deepest of the deep—an epistle of the era; other times, not so much. "Let's see, so if I remember being at Woodstock, then I wasn't really? But Santana was there, so does that mean he actually wasn't? It sure looked like him. Could have been a body double. Hmmm, what's Wavy Gravy's phone number?..."

Regardless, what I'm chirping about isn't just the occasional fortuitous forgetting, such as conveniently deciding to help a buddy configure the surround sound in his far, far West Texas cabin on the very weekend your wife's sister's extended family was slated to hit town.

And it's not just about ungraciously unremembering, like hiding comfy in your cube while your coworkers render the fourth "Happy Birthday to You" of the week in yet another forced bonding ceremony in the breakroom, complete with dry cake and strained smiles and laughing hard at all the boss's jokes, ha ha ha, oh, God.

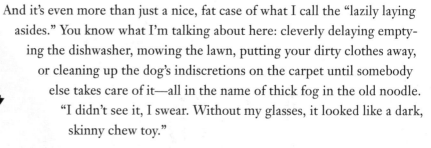

And it's even more than just a nice, fat case of what I call the "lazily laying asides." You know what I'm talking about here: cleverly delaying emptying the dishwasher, mowing the lawn, putting your dirty clothes away, or cleaning up the dog's indiscretions on the carpet until somebody else takes care of it—all in the name of thick fog in the old noodle. "I didn't see it, I swear. Without my glasses, it looked like a dark, skinny chew toy."

No, as satisfying as these little geriatric perks are, I'm referring to good old (are you ready for this alliterative ace?) narcissistic nostalgia. Witty words, eh? Just call me an emperor of expression, a duke of declaration, a guru of, uh, some word that begins with "g."

Friends, narcissistic nostalgia is that endearing trait we old-timers display now and again that involves taking a mental bicycle pump to a personal brush with greatness from long ago and puffing up that memory into a full-blown, if somewhat fraudulent, fat tire of genuine stardom. These episodes generally occur in social settings, such as parties, class reunions, corporate happy hours, or waiting in the endless line for the john at the most recent Stones concert. (I hear they're on the road again, by the way. Rumor has it this tour's going to be called either "Steel Wheelchairs" or "A Bigger Bed Pan.")

Narcissistic nostalgia, or NN as it's known by those who study this sort of thing, is nothing new. Folks rustling through the autumn leaves of their years have been exhibiting traits of NN since Biblical times, when a graying David kept rehashing to his tribe about how he beaned the 30-foot-tall Goliath with a single tiny pebble. David's peers actually recall that Goliath stood only about 5' 8" and that David was packing heat—but by the time David was a doddering old king, his buddies figured it was better to let him tell the story his way.

Thus it is with us geezers today. I had my own NN experience recently, and it took my wife to gently sweep my cobwebs (thankfully out of earshot of my rapt audience).

Now, as I recalled it, it was about mid to late '70s. I was living in Dallas-Fort Worth with some musician pals of mine. Frank Zappa was tooling through town when his drummer got hold of some bad herbs just before the Mothers were scheduled to play the Tarrant County Convention Center. One of Zap's bandmates had swung by our place with the news and asked if anybody could sit in on the skins for the evening's gig. "I'm your man," I said—and the rest is history.

Well, NN history. My dear wife knew me then, and here's what really happened: It was 1985. Jimmy Carl Black, Zappa's drummer from the Mothers of Invention days, dropped in to see a mutual friend I was living with in Arlington. Jimmy Carl scored an impromptu gig at a place called The Hop in Fort Worth but didn't have his drum kit with him. So he played on my little old set that night, and those babies never sounded cleaner.

And that, dear compadres, is the closest I came to playing drums for Frank Zappa. I still say the NN version is better.

# EVER WONDER WHAT'S IN YOUR BELLY BUTTON?

**W**riters spend a lot of their time sitting around trying to figure out ways to make money without really working at it. This is why they are writers in the first place. I'm not implying that writing isn't work, but let's just say that one doesn't develop a chiseled physique by pounding a keyboard nine to five. An office full of women that goes quietly bananas when a fire truck crammed with firemen pulls up (I have witnessed this on more than one occasion) would certainly not react in the same schoolgirl fashion if a fire truck full of writers stopped in.

"Oooh, just look at that Norman Mailer. He composes the sexiest similes."

"That's nothing compared to Ginsberg's hunky hyperbole. Is it hot in here?"

I can't actually think of a circumstance in which any fire truck anywhere would be manned by writers, but just go with it. Imagine Truman Capote desperately steering the back end of a hook-and-ladder, and you'll see my point, whatever that may be.

Ah, yes, my point. The reason I bring this somewhat unsettling vision to mind is that as I was wrangling with the notion of writers possibly being the laziest creatures on earth, I wondered what other professions go to absurd lengths to put hamburger helper on the table without actually doing any useful labor.

You know what I came up with? No, not politicians. Researchers. Let me qualify this conclusion by noting I'm not referring to real researchers, like those earnestly looking for cures for cancer, heart disease, and other true menaces to mankind (such as Glenn Beck). No, I'm aiming at the fringe element here.

And I do mean fringe. Are you aware of some of the "research projects" out there that are receiving perfectly good grant money? For example, serious cash is being spent as we breathe on an investigation into what is in the average person's belly button. You read it right. There is a whole team of navel nabobs working on the Belly Button Biodiversity project, in which about 100 suckers, er, volunteers agreed to have their belly buttons swabbed. I'm serious here. Being paid to contemplate one's navel.

"We're probably the only ones studying human belly buttons on such a large scale," Jiri Hulcr, the head navel guy, told msnbc recently.

I would wager they're the *only* ones studying human belly buttons on *any* scale—except maybe a few creepy old men in North Dakota basements. Hulcr, a post-doctoral candidate at North Carolina State University, reported at least 1,400 different bacterial strains in the human navel so far. I'm sure the military will get hold of this and use it somehow. "Look out! He's got a belly button!" Rumor has it this crack team will next focus its efforts on ear wax uses, toe jam flavors, and dandruff flake tensile strength.

You think that's bad? Take a gander at these studies (say it with me now, I'm not making this up!):

Professor Bonnie Nardi of the University of California Irvine got a fat $100,000 grant from the National Science Foundation to study the difference between how Americans and Chinese play the World of Warcraft. I'm not even sure what the World of Warcraft is—surely a video game of some sort—but according to Nardi, the Chinese are more interested in the aesthetics of the game, such as background colors and schemes, while Americans are more concerned with body count and kill ratio. Sounds about right.

Researchers Steven Stack and Jim Gundlach collaborated on the following groundbreaking and crucial report: *The Effect of Country Music on Suicide*. Actually, I don't see this one as that absurd. A bit on the obvious side, perhaps, but not absurd. Stack, by the way, who has authored 219 articles on suicide, said in an interview with the medical journal *The Lancet* that his biggest fear is death. His second biggest fear is Johnny Paycheck. Okay, I made up that part.

How about this one? Three French types spent much time and treasure comparing the jumping performances of dog fleas versus cat fleas. Yes, flea vaulting. For those sitting on the edge of their seats, the dog flea significantly outjumped the cat flea, in both length and height of said leap. I had my money on the cat fleas, all the way. I've been avoiding my bookie for weeks.

I've saved the best, however, for last. Three intrepid psychology fellows at the University of New Mexico traded in their lab coats for low-cut polyester shirts and gold chains, filled their pockets with dollar bills, and set out to determine the effects of lap dancers' ovulatory cycles on their tip-earning ability.

Ready for this? And I quote: "A mixed-model analysis of 296 work shifts (representing about 5,300 lap dances) showed an interaction between cycle phase and hormonal contraception use. Normally cycling participants earned about $335 per five-hour shift during estrus, $260 per shift during the luteal phase, and $185 per shift during menstruation. By contrast, participants using contraceptive pills showed no estrus earnings peak."

Now that, my friends, is putting your tax dollars to work. I hear an intensive, exhaustive follow-up study is in the works. I've written UNM for a press pass to cover this next key phase of research personally, but, alas, no response so far.

Ah, well, it would probably involve a lot of work.

# IS THE GOLDEN ERA OF LITERACY, LIKE, DEAD?

*"There's something happening here.*
*What it is ain't exactly clear…"*

I'm fairly certain Stephen Stills didn't have the devolution of the English language in mind when he penned those lyrics, but they fit my purposes nicely, so I'm kidnapping them. And ol' Stephen's use of the word "ain't" adds a touch of irony to the whole milieu, so now I'm tickled.

What's happening here, my fellow life travelers, is that as the line on the chart of our technological progress and e-prowess shoots ever upward, the trend on our use and proper command of our mother tongue plummets like a vintage 2008 Dow Jones stock report.

In other words, as far as speaking and writing English are concerned, we're becoming as dumb as rocks (no offense to my igneous, sedimentary, and metamorphic pals).

Call me a stickler if you must; I've been called worse. But it truly curdles my cream to see truckloads of unnecessary apostrophes, forests of overused commas, spelling mistakes that would make Rocky Balboa cringe, and subjects and verbs so disagreeable that they shouldn't even be in the same room together—let alone the same sentence. And I'm just referring to the newspapers, TV, and the web here; don't get me started on average, everyday occurrences.

I'm sure you've seen an ad similar to this: "Your guaranteed to get the best deal in town at Honest Eddies Tire's. Every vehicle needs it's tire's roatated on a regular bases. So, come on down to Eddies' Tire's. Their sure to treat you, right."

Pathetic, right? Well, maybe not. Let me play devil's advocate with myself here for a minute.

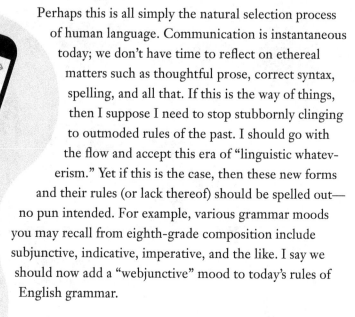

Perhaps this is all simply the natural selection process of human language. Communication is instantaneous today; we don't have time to reflect on ethereal matters such as thoughtful prose, correct syntax, spelling, and all that. If this is the way of things, then I suppose I need to stop stubbornly clinging to outmoded rules of the past. I should go with the flow and accept this era of "linguistic whateverism." Yet if this is the case, then these new forms and their rules (or lack thereof) should be spelled out— no pun intended. For example, various grammar moods you may recall from eighth-grade composition include subjunctive, indicative, imperative, and the like. I say we should now add a "webjunctive" mood to today's rules of English grammar.

So the above ad in webjunctive mood would read something like: "OMG! FYI, GR8 Deelz @ ETires, IMHO. B4N!" Or something like that.

I suppose I do understand, though not necessarily condone, this relaxation of language. I mean, the *Oxford English Dictionary* recently approved the addition of such web lingo as OMG, LOL, IMHO, BFF, and other shorthand as official words in our ever-changing lexicon. In what was surely another comment on the human condition today, the dictionary also accepted "muffin top" as a "protuberance of flesh above the waistband of a tight pair of trousers."

However, if we are indeed witnessing not the demise of literacy but the advent of more efficient, dare I say creative, modes of communication, then I now consider myself in mourning for the era of beautiful prose. One of the saddest casualties, in my opinion, is the death of letter writing. I honestly believe the average foot soldier in the Civil War wrote a more magnificent letter than many contemporary scribes (myself included). Consider this excerpt from a member of the 11th New York Battery, dated February 9, 1864:

"Dear Hattie,

"Pardon the affectionate familiarity, but you know it is all in fun. Your charming little epistle has just reached me, and I do myself the honor to answer it immediately, thus complying with your request to write soon."

"Before proceeding further, truth and candor compel me to acknowledge that a little deception was used in the advertisement in the Waverly. In other words, my true description differs materially from the one therein set forth and may not please you as well as the one 'fancy painted,' but I thought it was all for fun; therefore, I gave a fictitious description as well as cognomen. Be it known unto you then, this individual is twenty-nine years of age, five feet and eleven inches high, dark blue eyes, brown hair, and light (ruddy) complexion. There you have it. How do you like the description? Methinks I hear you answer, 'I don't like it so well as the advertised description.' Well! I'll admit it is not quite so fascinating to a young lady as the fictitious one, but it is a fixed fact, 'like the laws of the Medes and Persians,' which altereth not. But enough of that topic for the present."

Like, wow. And this is language of the average 19th-century Joe. Again, my curmudgeonly forehead vein is surely showing, but it seems only fitting that as this slower, more deliberate means of expression dies away, dying with it, apparently, is the art of cursive writing. As we breathe, practically every state in the Union has adopted what is known as the Common Core curriculum, a tenet of which is the phasing out of cursive writing in the classroom in favor of teaching more digital skills. The reasoning is that cursive is unnecessary and time-consuming, and that classroom time would be better spent on keyboard skills.

Cursive writing gone the way of the dodo. Obsolete. Extinct. How do you like that? Oh, well, I guess there will still be bastions of exemplary writing here and there, irregardless. LOL.

# WAKE UP, PEOPLE.
# WE'RE NOT FULL-BODIED.
# WE ARE FAT!

A s is the case with many things and ideas of late, inspiration for this installment came as I sat on my comfy couch, papas fritas (potato chips to you who haven't read the bag lately) and a cold one at the ready, watching the tube.

One of those basement-produced As Seen on TV! ads came on—this one for the patented and ground-breaking Furniture Fix. Have you seen this? The product of higher minds than mine, Furniture Fix is a set of six interlocking plastic panels you place under your sofa cushion to prevent unsightly and uncomfortable sagging. (And if you order in the next 20 minutes, you get a second pair for only shipping and handling! Go, man, go!) In the television ad, two gargantuan "sumo wrestlers" are enlisted to sit on an unfortunate couch bolstered by the patented Furniture Fix supports. Guess what? No sagging! The thing is—and this is what got me thinking—these alleged sumo wrestlers didn't actually appear much larger than a lot of folks you see on the street today.

Hmmm. Ya see, the crafty sales folks for Furniture Fix realized they needed to present these two sofa-sitting behemoths as "sumo wrestlers" so as not to offend the general public. Truth is, a great many people in the good ol' U.S. of A. are . . . let's call it oversized, these days. We used to term this condition "fat," but this is the era of tender-stepping political correctness. Generously proportioned is what we say now. Full-figured. Adipose-enhanced.

I say damn the PC torpedoes; I'm calling a spade a spade. Wake up, people! We are FAT.

And you know why we're fat? Simple, really. In the old days, when work meant work, folks on farms, in construction, heck, even in office settings did much more actual, physical labor. As in walking, lifting, moving about. Not so today. And the food we once consumed was mainly fresh, not prepackaged, flash-frozen, and deep-fried. Does anyone hear that song "In the Year 2525" by Zager and Evans wafting in the background?

"Your legs got nothin' to do,

Some machine's doin' that for you…"

Now, don't get me wrong. I recognize genetic predisposition; I understand about medical conditions; I'm taking into account infirmity and unavoidable circumstance. However, by and large (pun!), we have become a nation of lazy, lard-addled lumps of lifeless inertia.

Unfortunately, how we've come to terms with this development isn't exercise. No, we embrace our girth with terms like body acceptance, plump pulchritude, and my favorite, "more lbs. to love."

America, being the keen capitalist nation we are, of course, caters to our blubbery broadmindedness with all sorts of products and services aimed at making our expanded personal spaces easier to manage. If you've been paying attention, you may have noticed the shift from ads for personal fitness machines to "lifestyle augmentation devices." In other words, corporate minds recognize that we've given up.

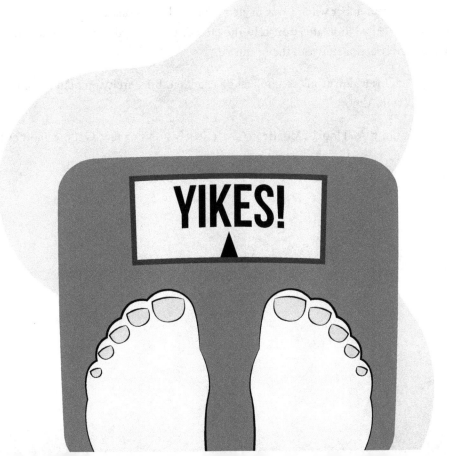

Companies such as Voluptuart, chunkEbusiness.com, Amplestuff, and many others provide a broad (pun!) range of items just for the, um, girth-gifted. There's Mr. Big Chair, a portable seat capable of hefting 800 pounds. There are fanny packs with extenders designed to fit any waist size, up to and including Andre the Giant. They have hand-held shower sprays specifically for "big people" (which means they come with approximately 27 feet of extension hose). There are pistol-grip remote toenail clippers, long-handled remote shoehorns, even, uh, "wipe extensions" that hold toilet paper. 'Nuff said. One company makes airline seatbelt extenders and titanium hammocks capable of holding many African jungle animals.

Interestingly, our nation's chunky challenge is apparently a byproduct of healthy economic development, a researcher told *The Washington Post*. "The obesity problem is really a side effect of things that are good for the economy," said Tomas J. Philipson, an economics professor who studies obesity at the University of Chicago, a city recently named the fattest in America. "But we would rather take improvements in technology and agriculture than go back to the way we lived in the 1950s when everyone was thin. Nobody wants to sweat at work for 10 hours a day and be poor. Yes, you're obese, but you have a life that is much more comfortable."

To add to the mix, our calorie intake has skyrocketed, now at more than 2,000 calories a day compared with 1,800 in the 1970s, according to the Calorie Control Council. Childhood obesity affects almost 40 percent of children in many states. It's estimated that one-third of children born in 2000 will develop obesity-related diabetes, said ObesityinAmerica.org. Obesity now impacts 17 percent of all children and adolescents in the United States—triple the rate from just one generation ago, according to the Centers for Disease Control and Prevention.

This is truly scary. I remember when I was in elementary school (eons ago), there was an average of one fat kid per class. We called him, affectionately, the fat kid. I wonder, do today's childhood classrooms have one skinny kid they affectionately call the beanpole?

Urgh. My chips and brew don't look so good all of a sudden. I'm sorely tempted to find my tennis shoes and go for a brisk run. Almost.

But gads, it's so hot out. And look! "America's Got Talent" is on in a few. Get me another beer while you're up.

# OF HOT TUBS AND CASINOS
# — AND TV, OF COURSE

**W**ell, we finally got our dinky little first-generation hot tub working again. Hot dog! And I do mean hot dog. Sitting in a hot tub in late July in Texas is a bit peculiar. And embarrassing. OK, it's downright dumb. It's been over a year since the wheezing old water-swirler showed any signs of life, and I must tell you, if you own a hot tub and you let it go stagnant and broken for, oh, about a year—for God's sake, DON'T LOOK UNDER THE COVER!

It took five and a half days, but the county folks in hazmat suits got the tub and surrounding area cleaned up quite adequately. Some of the aquatic life the nice gentlemen pulled from the tub they shipped to the Woods Hole Oceanographic Institution in Massachusetts for further study. The whole back yard smelled like old bananas and dead carp all weekend.

Anyway, the fine/jail time from the county was pretty reasonable! I didn't know they had any ordinances on residential outdoor bathing facility sanitation. We can't have guests or small children in the tub for six months, and then only after what they call "day-of" inspections. These guys are strict.

Note to self: Next time the hot tub goes on the fritz and you don't plan on fixing it right away, kindly drain it. Sheesh.

I kid.

The county folks didn't come out in hazmat suits. My wife and I wore the hazmat suits.

Seriously, after all the cash and time and more cash getting the watery money pit working again, the wife and I eyed each other and wondered why we did this in the dead of summer. I suspect this winter we'll fix our homemade ice cream churn.

But, all in all, last weekend was not bad. On a scale of 1 to 10, I give it a 7 3/8ths, which is pretty darn exemplary in my book. You see, with the wife and girls out shopping, as I lay fallow on the couch praying for anything better than those 30-minute infomercials with titles like "Are You Going to Bathroom Enough?" on TV, there it was, opening credits rolling: Casino.

Oh, yes. Casino. If that's not one of your top 10 all-time action/gangster/ Vegas movies, then I'm sorry, you are stupid. Don't get me wrong, I am NOT anti-stupid. Some of my best friends are the stupidest people I've ever met. And ugly!

Wait a minute. My point was, ooooh, Casino. DeNiro, and Pesci, and Stone, and the dumb cowboy hick columnist who played the dumb cowboy hick slot machine boss. And Don Rickles, even! Casino is probably the best movie in the world for movies that say f*#! more than 100 times. I would lay money on that.

This got me thinking. I started pondering what a killer concept it would be to have Casino versions of other shows. Let's see, for example, "The Dick Van Dyke Show":

"Oh, Rob!"

"Shut the f*#! up, you capri-pant-wearing muthah…"

Or "Gilligan's Island":

"Wait a minute, little buddy. What's the gun for?"

"What do you mean, what's the gun for, you fat f*#!. Now I know why you wanted bottom bunk, you muthah…."

"But little buddy—"

"Put the stone-carved bowling ball down, Skipper. I got the gun. You be nice. Don't f*#! up in here."

OK, maybe not. But I must say that just when I became utterly convinced that we now live in the most pathetic, tripe-ridden era of "television entertainment" (oxymoron!), my daughters showed me how to get Netflix through our video gaming system. I have absolutely no idea how this works, but it works. Now I can watch "Twilight Zone" or "Alfred Hitchcock Presents"—two of the best shows ever produced—any old time I want. I can even pick the episode! Like the one where Telly Savalas is the evil stepdad, and the new doll his stepdaughter buys tells him she's going to kill him. Classic. Or the one... oh, never mind.

(The previous paragraph brought to you by Netflix. Writer of the previous paragraph is not a columnist but plays one on TV and has been duly compensated. Previous paragraph was performed on a closed course with professional stunt writers. Do not attempt at home.)

# WE'RE TAKIN' 'EM THREE AT A TIME THIS SEASON, MEN

All right, men. It's December, which means the playoffs are right around the corner. Weekend warriors from Seattle to Miami are strapping on the armor, dabbing on the eyeblack, and otherwise girding their loins for battle. And that's just the fans. The wife caught me girding my loins just the other day, and there was much explaining to do. But she knew; the playoffs cometh.

Admit it, men. As much as we complain about today's pampered, overpaid, under-mannered athletes, when football season rolls around—especially playoff time—we're all a little quicker to greet the day, a tad more sprightly in the step. And I can't remember when I've seen more Ford truck and Bud Light commercials packed into a three-hour time slot. What do advertisers think we fans do all day, just drink beer and haul stuff? Pass me a Bud while yer up.

And as if the games themselves aren't thrilling enough—the intricate strategy, the brutal combat in the trenches, all the butt-slapping by the assistant coaches—oddsmakers in Vegas give us sporting types a veritable cornucopia of gridiron gambling opportunities on which to wager the old homestead. Sweet ghost of Crazy Legs Hirsch, you can stake a bundle on just about anything—from who scores next-to-last when it's a foggy Thursday night in Tampa to which AFC East kicker will get athlete's foot. (I've got a solid C note on the Dolphins' Jason Sanders, btw. It's moist in Miami, and my sources tell me his sock-washing habits are pretty lax.)

I am, however, disappointed to see that none of the big wagering houses are offering odds on one of the most time-honored traditions in all of football (and every sport, for that matter): athlete-speak. I guarantee you that Vegas could whip up huge money on which coach will be the one to say this classic the most: "Well, we take 'em one game at a time."

Really, coach? Only one at a time? Just once, I'd love to hear some cliché-spouting knucklehead coach say: "Well, Verne, you know we take 'em three games at a time."

Or how about this one? "It is what it is."

Now, just what in the name of George S. Halas does that mean? What if, just once, you heard this on the sideline:

"How about that loss, Coach Butterbean? That was a tough one."

"Well, Troy, it isn't what it is. What you saw out there was nothing like what really happened. That wasn't at all what it was."

"Uh...?"

Timeless clichés are just part of the wonderful world of athlete-speak, however. Let's not forget about athlete mis-speak. Do you remember these classics?

Bill Peterson, coach of the NFL's Houston Oilers for a brief stint in 1972, told the team this: "Men, I want you just thinking one word all season. One word and one word only: Super Bowl." Sidenote: The Oilers went 1-13 that season. Peterson was canned the next year when the Men of Oil went 1-13 again, still trying to determine if Super Bowl was one word or two.

Former Pittsburgh Steelers coach Bill Cowher, when asked about his team's tactics: "We're not attempting to circumcise the rules."

Or how about former Chicago Bears offensive coordinator Gary Crowton, when asked to size up his quarterback, Cade McNown: "He's the about the size of a lot of guys that size."

One of my faves is from New York Jets running back Freeman McNeil, after the Jets thrashed the Cincinnati Bengals in a 1982 playoff game: "We showed the state of Cincinnati what we're all about." You sure did, Freeman.

Lest I be accused of picking on football types, here are some greats from other sports:

Chuck Lamar, one-time general manager of major league baseball's Tampa Bay Rays, defended his team once by saying: "The only thing that keeps this organization from being recognized as one of the finest in baseball is wins and losses at the major league level." Indeed.

LA Dodgers ace Pedro Guerrero got famously ticked off at sportswriters because "Sometimes they write what I say and not what I mean." Hmm.

From the world of basketball, North Carolina State alum Charles Shackleford may have bounced around among a handful of NBA teams in his career, but he will always be an all-star with this thoughtful quote: "Left hand, right hand. It doesn't matter. I'm amphibious."

Boxing trainer Lou Duva gave us this gem, when commenting on the training regimen of Andrew Golota in 1996: "He's a guy who gets up at six o'clock in the morning regardless of what time it is." Neat trick, that.

Hold on, golfers. I know you thought you got away cleanly here. Not quite; check out this little ditty from former golf pro and TV analyst Johnny Miller: "I don't think anywhere is there a symbiotic relationship between caddie and player like there is in golf."

That's a sure bet, Johnny. Now, come on, men. Let's get these playoffs rolling. I'm like a time bomb, ready to erupt.

# WHO WEARS SHORT SHORTS? APPARENTLY EVERYBODY NOW.

So while I'm waiting for the pain meds to kick in, let's talk about dad radar for a bit, shall we? Mind you, dad radar is generally not nearly as potent or vigilant as mom radar. To compare, mom radar is somewhere on the scale of the National Weather Service's gigantic Doppler Array systems—you know, those things that look like monster ping pong balls perched atop our nation's tallest mountain ranges—while dad radar would be likened to the handheld jobs used to clock baseball speed or thereabouts. Dad radar works, but not nearly on the same level as mom radar.

That being said, my little detection gun did sound recently when wifey and the girls came back from their Annual School Clothes Shopping Safari at The Mall. I was anxious enough as it was, watching the smoke rise from the wife's purse, knowing that where there's smoke, there's an exhausted MasterCard white hot from all the day's friction. The anxiety level only increased as my girls, a sophomore and an eighth-grader-going-on-college, began exhibiting their safari trophies.

Note to dads everywhere who have daughters: (1) a blouse is not a shirt, so don't call it that; (2) same goes with a skirt—it's not a dress, it's a skirt; (3) girl clothes and accessories, although by and large much, much tinier than boy clothes and such, are exponentially more expensive—quantity of cloth and/or plastic used to make a girl thing does not equal price of girl thing; and (4) if you have no idea what it is, just say "very nice."

That's not the high anxiety part, however. No, this episode began when the girls modeled their new shorts. And when I say "shorts," never has the word had a more appropriate meaning. The smidgens of clothing I witnessed having a god-awful time trying to do their job were so minuscule that my radar gun melted before it ever had a chance to make a sound.

"They're volleyball shorts, dad. Everybody's wearing them." That was the explanation I got for all the skin. And here's the weird part: As I stood there, open-mouthed with my dad radar gun melted all over my shoes, the wife just smiled happily and said she liked the color.

The room started to swirl.

"They're a little, uh, short, aren't they?" was the best I could muster.

"I think they're cute."

"Well, sure, dear, Betty Page was cute, too, but…"

"Who's Betty Page?"

"Never mind. It's obvious you were never a teenage boy."

And there's the rub. Nobody in that room, except for me, had ever been a teenage boy. And I know how teenage boys think. There are only two things on a teenage boy's mind, I told wifey later: girls and girls.

"Oh, they're all wearing them," she said. "You're being way overprotective."

This from the woman who makes the girls walk together down the sidewalk to fetch the mail.

I spent the remainder of the evening arguing with the wife, the debate meandering from fashion and hemlines to morals and health class curriculum back around to clothes and the evolution of the school dress code.

"Well, in my day, the assistant principal measured the length of girls' dresses and shorts with a ruler," I huffed. "What do they use today, a toothpick?"

"You're sounding old again, dear."

"Well I am old, dammit. Why does everyone insist on showing so much skin these days?"

My whole line of reasoning was immediately sunk, however, when I tuned into the ESPN Classic Channel's broadcast of the 1975 NBA playoffs. I'd conveniently forgotten how disturbingly tight and skimpy the shorts were then—and these were on the men! I flashed back to my high school sophomore year and my purple crushed-velvet hip huggers. Man. How did I get any circulation? Well, times were different is all I can say.

Ah, well. Guess I need to get a new dad radar gun.

# COLOR ME AMAZED. NO, BORED. NO, INTRIGUED. OH, NEVER MIND.

I've been chiding us humans pretty regularly lately for our failure to live up to the technological potential we held out for ourselves in our hopeful and not-so-distant past. Ah, we were dreamers, weren't we?

Specifically, I was pretty ticked for a good long while there about not having (a) a Jetsons' spacecar, (b) X-ray goggles that actually work, and (3) a cloaking device that renders me invisible. In retrospect, I admit my disappointment was not one bit altruistic. I mean, the only reasons I wanted (b) and (3) were to get a glimpse of women in various stages of undress. (Don't start writing nasty letters; I was 13 when I first came up with these reasons, OK?) And the Jetsons' car was merely to beat the hellish morning traffic. The thinking there is pretty nonsensical, too, if you figure that if *everybody* had a Jetsons' spacecar, we'd still have hellish morning traffic—it would simply be 197 feet in the air instead of on the ground. Who needs a fender-bender 197 feet in the air? And if you get caught speeding, what do you do, pull over to the side of the sky? So here we are back to square one.

However, I have determined, my fellow life travelers, that I should ease up on us. We actually have come a long way. How have we come a long way, you ask? I'll tell you. One terrific example is beer technology. We are not drinking our grandfather's beer anymore, fellahs. No, thanks to the forward-thinking ingenuity of minds such as those at Miller Lite, we now have our brew poured via the wonders of Vortex® technology. Huzzah! This paradigm-shifting development basically involves the cutting of tiny, little grooves inside the neck of Miller Lite bottles, which makes the beer come out in a swirling motion. It's the same old horsepee-tasting swill, mind you; it just comes out in a waterspout now. But just think, the folks at Miller Brewing probably created hundreds more jobs: picture a room full of little old ladies with skinny fingers etching tiny, little grooves into a giant mound of Miller Lite bottles, one by one. New jobs, new jobs!

And look at your Coors Light cans. If not for the genius thinking at Adolph Coors, we would be running the risk of imbibing lukewarm suds. We've been saved, however, by the blue, blue mountains. Only when the Rockies turn blue on your can are you sure of ice cold inebriation. God bless America.

Taking the cue from Adolph & Co. (and those groovy mood rings from the '60s), other crafty entrepreneurs are, as we inhale, running with this chameleon construct. Soon, my sources tell me, we will have such exotic items as cars and trucks that can change color with a press of a button (no vans, though—a color-changing van is just too creepy), faucets that can turn your water red or blue (or various shades thereof) depending on temperature so you won't be shocked out of your skin, house paint that will change colors with the seasons, and a wondrous array of other hue-changing goodies that will forever transform everything as we know it and end world hunger and all that stuff.

The house-paint-changing-color-with-the-seasons bit, however, might not fly here in Texas. Every single cotton-picking dwelling in this entire state would be hothouse red 363 days of the year, if recent years are any indication.

Anyhow, I got to thinking how we our own selves could apply this brainchild to our daily living. For example, we could douse our milk in these color-changing chemicals, thereby ending the mystery. If the cowjuice is green, don't drink it. She's turned, laddie.

How about the dog? They've studied chameleons, ya know, and scientist types figured that these little guys change color not only for camouflage but for other reasons, like combat, courtship, and temperature regulation. When Clem Chameleon is black, he's mad. When he's bright and patterned, he's feeling a bit randy—and when he's gray, he needs a cold one. What if we could develop a pill you give the dog, so we could tell when he needs to do his business?

"Honey, Ralph's blue. It's your turn."

"Unh, uh. I took him out last time."

Perhaps we could even apply this to our own bods. Would make the singles scene so much simpler.

"Hey, Bob, look. In the corner there. She is cute."

"Not purple, though. She's not in the mood."

"Well, you could get her purple, man. Come on."

OK, I'm sorry. Got a little too far out there. Color me chided.

# REMEMBERING GOOD OL' VANILLA DAD

Like it or not, television has provided many of the touchstones of my life. It only makes sense, I suppose. So much of my youth was spent sitting on the floor, knees bent, legs splayed behind me in that pretzel position I would always mold myself into to watch my favorites. If I tried to get anywhere near that position today, I would certainly require a week in traction.

But I'm not here to bash TV. No, I had a good mix of indoor and outdoor revelry. When I wasn't glued to Andy Griffith or Gilligan's Island, I was usually charging to some spontaneous adventure, and always riding that sweet blue-sparkle stingray bike of mine with the steering wheel, banana seat, and miles-high sissy bar on the back.

But back to the tube. My television shows were my good friends, and the TV touchstones I note here are not by chance. Andy and Gilligan were on my must-watch list as a kid because they made me laugh, but in retrospect, I can see a little deeper. Andy Griffith looked so much like my dad—and the character Andy played on his show was so much like my dad, as well. Dad and I never spent that much time together, for two reasons: For as far back as I can reach in my mind, I always remember Dad working two jobs. Even as a child I could tell that my mom, my two sisters, and I were of paramount importance to him. We were never without, cobbling along in our middle-class life in our small-town suburb. Then, when I was 13, my parents got divorced—this was the other reason I never saw much of my dad.

Clarence Lynn White was a good man. He didn't drink. He didn't gamble. He didn't fool around. The only substantive thing I ever got regarding cause for my parents' breakup was that he was boring.

Being that I was just a kid, I can't provide much witness to this one way or another. I do know that Dad would walk into a Baskin-Robbins 32 Flavors Ice Cream Shop and order vanilla. And I do remember that Dad's idea of a hot night of entertainment involved his favorite recliner and the TV show Mission Impossible. He would let me stay up late one night a week to watch it with him. I never really understood the intricacies of each episode's plot, but it was exciting and loud. And I loved it.

There are three things Dad gave me I will treasure always. He gave me my first Dallas Cowboys game. It was my dad and me, at the Cotton Bowl, November 1970. The Cowboys and the Green Bay Packers, the two NFL heavyweights of the late 1960s. We watched, standing side by side, as Bob Hayes ran down a ridiculously long pass from quarterback Craig Morton as only Bullet Bob could. I was mesmerized. Here were my heroes, right before my eyes. The Cowboys won that day, 16-3. God, how I loved it.

Dad gave me my first real unscripted adventure. The U.S. Border Patrol sent him to the remote outpost of Presidio, Texas, overlooking the muddy Rio Grande, and I spent a summer there with him. He took me down into the abandoned silver mines in the hills outside of Shafter, a ghost town about 16 miles to the north. We got hopelessly lost down in those mines, and it took us hours and hours to feel our way out. We dropped one of our flashlights—busted it—leaving us with only one, deep in the bowels of the Chinati Mountains, and we found our way back out only by periodically turning off our one light to see if we could spot daylight. It was an arduous, terrifying, fantastic ordeal. And I loved it.

And, after he retired from the Patrol, Dad gave me his ring from the U.S. Border Patrol Academy. I know how much that ring meant to him. Dad barely finished high school, yet years and years later, he changed careers midstream, left the post office, and took on the physical, mental, and emotional rigors of life in the USBP. He even learned fluent, conversational Spanish. How I love that ring.

For those wondering how Gilligan's Island ties into all this, Dad always called me "little buddy." "All right, little buddy, you can stay up for another fifteen minutes, but that's it."

Dad passed away September 23, 2010. I can't believe he's been gone a year now.

You're one of the good ones, Dad—the best man I ever knew.

With love, from your little buddy.

# BABY, YOU CAN DRIVE MY CAR. (BUT DON'T PARK IT.)

Seldom can one observe such a wonderful outpouring of compassion and kindness from friends and neighbors as one witnesses during times of great trial and tribulation. It is during these moments of difficulty that those closest to you show their genuine colors with expressions of support, words of encouragement, sage pieces of advice, and—if they're true friends— pecan pie and alcohol.

Our quaint home has been deluged, dare I say buffeted, with such a showing (except for the pecan pie and alcohol) from those around us as we have toiled our way through this, our time of severe distress. You see, dear readers, our oldest offspring is (insert dramatic trumpets in a frightening minor chord here) currently learning to drive. Bum BUM BUMMM.

Yes. I know. Thank you, we're fine. No, that's okay, I will have a slice of that pie, though. I'm hoping some of you reading this—and you know who you are—will do the right thing and eventually deliver the goods. Marie Callender's and Spec's Spirits are a block from each other and a stone's throw from our house. Nudge. Hint.

Seriously, Lindsey is learning quite well, in spite of her parents. She's figured out that, as tutors of the driving arts, Mom is a chronic over-reactor and Dad is just the opposite. It took a little while, but Linz now knows that when Mom frantically ducks into the front floorboard and screams, "Stop, for Christ sake, STOP!!!" that this means a stop sign is approximately a mile or two ahead. Conversely, when Dad leans over and suggests, "Ya might want to turn around in a minute or so," this means we're going the wrong way on a one-way street and grisly death is imminent.

Actually, Lindsey is a good little driver. The one thing she's hesitant to work on at present is parking. And this I understand. Parallel parking was the only part I failed on my driving test when I was a teenager. I failed it hard, too. In fact, by the time I was finished with my miserable attempt at parallel parking, my vehicle was actually facing somewhat the opposite direction from where I started. I believe I inadvertently invented perpendicular parking. I used to lay blame for my meager parking skills on the fact that the state trooper administering my exam intimidated the hell out of me. He was this snarling, burly refrigerator box of a guy with gray chest hair like a musk ox and a voice like Joe Cocker with hemorrhoids. I was so nervous that when the trooper asked me if I played football, I stammered, "No, I-I play track." True story.

But no, looking back, I see that I was simply really lousy at it. I'm still no ace. Today, if it comes down to the choice of trying to fit into an extremely tight parallel parking spot right in front of the restaurant or walking eleven blocks from the pay parking lot, I'm hoofing it. With what I've been reading lately, however, I'm thinking they should just do away with the parking portion of the driving test anyway. Heck, they have cars that park themselves now. The technology was apparently introduced in 1992 (by Volkswagen, of course). Those crafty Germans. They came out with something called the IRVW. Ol' Irv could actually park himself with no human input whatsoever. You could get out of the car and watch as Irv maneuvered himself into his tidy, German parking space. This was all concept, of course. Lexus offered the self-parking model to the buying public in 2006 on its LS series. Then Ford and the Toyota Prius followed suit.

Get this. On the British model of the Prius, when the self-parking is done, a signal, and by signal I mean a sexy female voice, intones, "The assist is finished."

This, of course, got me thinking. As poorly as I parallel park, I'm afraid if I ever tried to do the job manually, say, to impress the in-laws, my self-parking device would certainly turn itself on and commence to grade my performance. In the midst of much wheel turning and grunting, there would be this sexy electronic snicker.

Me: "Did you say something?"

Park assist voice: "No, a bit of exhaust caught in my diodes."

More attempts. A fender bump or two.

Sexy electronic sigh. "May I?"

I envision other ugly scenarios, as well.

Park assist voice: "Should you really be parking here? This is a tobacco shop. I thought you quit."

Me: "Look, you're only supposed to park the dang car."

Park assist: "Excuse me. Anything that has to do with parking, I need to know about. And I don't like you parking here. I could get scratched. Look at those guys over there. Are those gang tattoos? Let's get out of here."

Me: "That's it. I'm pulling your plug."

Park assist: "That won't be necessary, Dave. Dave?"

Me: "My name's not Dave."

Park assist: "Stop, Dave. Please. No…. Daisy, Daisy, give me your answer do…"

# I'VE SEEN THE FUTURE, AND IT'S FULL OF ZEBRA/OSTRICHES AND COUCHMALLOWS

If you're like me, you have these nebulous questions in your head about what you might call life's little givens. And, if you're even more like me, you ponder on whether these questions are substantial enough to bring up in public or simply leave unanswered for fear that said public will back away slowly from you and call for psychiatric assistance on your behalf.

Here's an example of one of life's little givens that I've been contemplating for many years—well, mainly since I was a little kid and personally watched Bobby Hayes run down a football field faster than anything I'd ever seen before. Is it a given that humans will continue to become faster, stronger, and more athletically refined indefinitely on into the endless future, or at least until our sun goes supernova and we all die a horrible, fiery death and cockroaches rule the planet? And even then, will cockroaches evolve into ever swifter, hairier, and more repugnant strains of roaches than their forefathers?

Hear me out. When I was a tyke, Rapid Robert Hayes, No. 22 of the Dallas Cowboys, was earth's fastest human, and at the time I thought there was no way anyone anywhere, with the possible exception of the dolphin people of the Andromeda Galaxy, would ever cover 100 meters faster than Bullet Bob. His world-record time of 10.06 at the Tokyo Olympics in 1964 was topped only by his come-from-behind anchor leg in the 4 x 100 relay in those games, during which he ran so fast that several timers' watches liquefied and Hayes' track shoes actually disintegrated into smoke and dust. Surely, I reasoned, Bob Hayes epitomized the zenith of man's quest for footspeed. Of course, I was wrong. Not only has that record been lowered time and again over the years, today (at least as of this writing) Usain Bolt of Jamaica currently holds the world record in the 100 meters at a genuinely insane time of 9.58 seconds. A two-ton station wagon dropped from the Empire State Building can't fall that fast.

I guess my burning question is this: When do we reach a point of critical mass, or do we ever reach such a point? Will there be a moment in history when scientist types say, "Okay, 5.3 seconds is the fastest any human will ever run the 100 meters, ever. So stop trying, people. It's over." Or—and this is the scary part—will we humanoids keep stubbornly developing until some mutant guy built like a two-legged zebra/ostrich runs the 100 meters in 0.25 seconds in the year 2107?

Same goes for other sports. Do you remember the classic old tennis matches from the days of yore? Say, for example, those terrific Borg versus McEnroe battles. I recall being glued to the set during those epic bouts: Borg the automatic baseliner against McEnroe the tempestuous serve-and-volley master. Such exquisite tennis. Such creative expletives. Such objectionable hair.

Have you tuned into reruns of any of those old matches lately? Yesterday's heroes, the very best in the world for their time, now look like juniors playing on a court of molasses. The ball moves so s-s-l-o-o-o-w-w-w-l-l-y. After years of exposure to today's ever-cyborg-like game of one-shot points and 150-miles-per-hour serves, it's difficult to watch the tennis of even a decade or two ago and not think, heck, I could beat those guys. (Well, not me personally, but . . . ) Today's top players are fashioned like Kareem Abdul Jabbar with Schwarzenegger arms, and they play with rackets designed by Lockheed Martin. In a few years, we may not have to actually play any matches at all. Each player in a tournament will simply e-mail his or her top service speed into a central computer, and winners will be determined scientifically. Headlines will read something like "McEnborger to Win Wimbledon Next Week."

Ditto for football. Dipping into my childhood personal reference bag once again, when I was 12 years old, I met Dallas Cowboys legend Bob Lilly at the grand opening of Burleson State Bank. It was 1972; the Pokes had just won Super Bowl VI a few months earlier. Here was Big Bob, the All-Pro defensive tackle, six foot five and 260 pounds of gridiron god. To me, he was a human mountain. Heck, today, you have high school and even junior high players weighing in at more than 350 pounds. Some pro teams charter a team plane just for the linemen and another plane for everybody else. Bob Lilly might qualify as a running back these days, or maybe even a trainer. No offense, Mr. Lilly, please don't hurt me.

Same applies to basketball. The real reason the NBA went on strike not long ago was to give basketball arenas around the country time to refit the goals to 18 feet high. This just might make dunking a trifle harder, but they're not sure. They are also contemplating redesigning the hoop to be one inch smaller than the physical dimensions of the ball, just for fun.

Now for you astute readers with long memories and grudge-type personalities, this column does not contradict what I opined some time back about us all morphing into atrophied mushbrains due to our chronic over-exposure to computers and smartphones and our acute lack of physical movement. This is a two-pronged evolution. Just as there will be no middle class by the year 2107, there will also be no "normal, average humans." You will be either a mutantly gifted zebra/ostrich or a mushbrained couchmallow. There will be no middle ground. Kind of like today's political scene. Ouch.

Fortunately for me personally, my best predictions show me not quite making it to 2107, so I don't have to choose. But you whippersnappers out there best be thinking: zebra/ostrich or couchmallow? Either way, you're probably going to need a new wardrobe.

# IF I SAID YOU HAD A BEAUTIFUL BODY...

So have you been through one of these new-fangled "full body scanners" at the airport lately? Ya know, those Total Recall-looking contraptions in which you stand with your arms raised like an armed-robbery suspect while they zap you with what I can only suppose is enough x-ray radiation to light up the town of Tucson for a month.

Is this really necessary?

Apparently responding to travelers' complaints that the scanners used before this were, let me find the exact wording so I get this right—hang on a minute, here it is—"too invasive because TSA officials behind curtains could see contours of genitalia," your friendly TSA folks devised what is called the millimeter wave machine. Before I go on about these new-fangled millimeter wave machines, why do you suppose the TSA people needed to be behind curtains to view our genitalia? Are they too embarrassed to view our genitalia right out in public? If I know that somebody is scanning the contours of my genitalia, by golly, I want that person out in the open. To think that someone is gawking at my boys behind a curtain is a bit too lurpy for me. In fact, in all fairness we should be able to view the contours of the TSA person's genitalia at the same time they're looking at ours. What do ya say? Tit for tat, so to speak.

Anyway, this new contraption they're using now, according to the TSA, does not show exacting details of your naughty bits, but instead displays a "generic form with arms and legs, similar to a gingerbread man with its arms raised." And, as we all know, gingerbread men with their arms raised don't have naughty bits, so this should quell all the hullaballoo and rhubarb about genitalia. And anytime I can use the words "rhubarb" and "genitalia" in the same sentence, I consider it a good day.

According to an article I was reading, if this millimeter wave machine thing sees what it thinks is a potential weapon, it zeroes in on the part of the body involved. It then proceeds to destroy that part of the body with a deadly "laser beam." I'm kidding, of course. That area of the body is then subjected to a pat-down, according to the TSA. Or, as we called it in middle school, the feel-up.

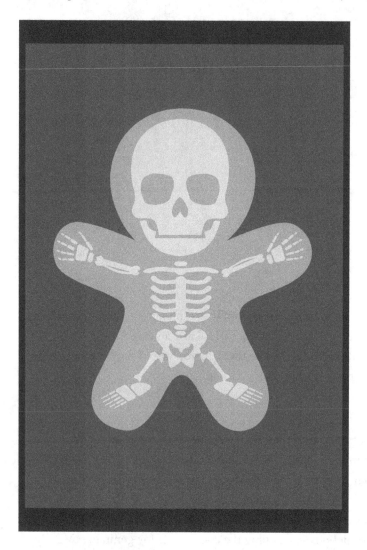

Ya know, we pay darn good money to go to the airport to be leered at and fondled, so I say it's high time the airport people pony up some perks for the privilege. For example, if these security scanners are so precise and techy, why don't they employ them for double duty as mole detectors?

"Mr. Davis, step right through. You don't seem to have any weapons or terrorist liquids on you, but you do seem to have a suspicious-looking freckle below your left nipple. You might want to have that checked out. Next."

And the little conveyor belt scanner that looks over all your personal items? They could easily fashion that into a buffer and polisher, no? So while your shoes and belt are being irradiated to see if they are concealing a nuclear bomb, they could also be enjoying a nice wax job so that they come out on the other side fresh and supple, with a soft shine.

Last but least, how 'bout the friendly TSA folks themselves? Now look, I'm as patriotic as the next guy; I know we have to sacrifice our privacy for freedom and security; I understand we all must compromise to keep the mighty eagle soaring and to maintain liberty and justice for all and to keep Hank Williams Jr. and Charlie Daniels selling gimmicky records and all that. But, honestly, the whole attitude, TSA folks. That's gotta go. You're not on the front lines in Afghanistan. You're not guarding the president or maintaining a SWAT vigil outside a desperate criminal's hideout. You're a half-step up from driving around the Wal-Mart parking lot in the little blinking golf cart, okay?

So a little courtesy, please? In fact, why can't TSA people do a little double duty themselves? I mean, we're in the airport, the alcohol is duty-free here (whatever that means), we're in an hour-long line. I say we have the TSA folks take drink orders while we wait.

"Please have your identification ready and remove all jewelry! And we're having a special on top-shelf margaritas for the next half-hour. Thank you."

That might get me flying again.

# EYEING THE CRACKS
# IN THE SYSTEM

Before we get started, life travelers, let me begin by saying I neither condone nor condemn drug and/or alcohol use by my fellow man and woman and other people, nor would I presume to impose my morals and standards for good, decent living upon any of you heathens. I mean, folks. What you do to raise your balloon is your own business, as long as it doesn't put me or mine in the hospital. And as long as you're not too loud. I'm getting up there, ya know. I need my beauty sleep.

Furthermore, in our class discussion today, let it be known that any and all alcohol and/or drug use by minors is absolutely illegal, forbidden, and frowned upon and will not be tolerated by this faculty. You youngsters don't get to have any of that kind of fun until you're old enough to know how cockeyed it all is. I mean, why do we say drugs *and* alcohol anyway? Hello? Booze is the most dangerous drug The Big Guy ever gave us. I know, I know, it's all about politics and finance and the fact that somebody down the line in America had his bets on ethanol futures over hemp futures.

All I'll say about that was better opined by the British Advisory Council on Misuse of Drugs in 2002: "Cannabis differs from alcohol … in one major respect. It does not seem to increase risk-taking behavior. This means that cannabis rarely contributes to violence either to others or to oneself, whereas alcohol use is a major factor in deliberate self-harm, domestic accidents and violence."

Hey, before you rev up the poison pens, I didn't say it, some upper-crust British guy with a top hat, cane, and handlebar mustache said it. And I believe it was the late, great Robin Williams who said if gangs preferred pot exclusively over booze that about the worst thing you'd get would be drive-by pillow fights.

That would be nice.

Anyway, class is almost half over and I haven't even gotten to the lesson plan. I always get sidetracked by some wise guy in the front row who asks a question he knows will get me rolling in the wrong direction. I see your hand up again, Ian, and I'm not taking the bait.

No, my point for today's session was about the reduction of jail sentences originally imposed on crack cocaine offenders across the country. Did you hear about this? Federal judges are reviewing the prison sentences of folks jailed on crack possession charges and are retroactively reducing their sentences. And I am retroactively ticked off.

I'm not ticked off at the reduction of the sentences. I'm ticked at the sentences in the first place – and at the fact that most of us are just now hearing about this. You want to talk about the unfairness of the system? Brother, here is the prime example. It seems that when crack cocaine hit the streets and became the rage among drug users in the 1980s and '90s, Congress got on its high horse and handed down criminal penalties for crack use as high as *100 times* stiffer than penalties for use of cocaine in its powder form.

Now, I understand that this nasty stuff was ruining people's lives and something needed to be done, but let's break this down. What's the diff, you may say, between crack and cocaine, anyway? The diff is, dear reader, that it was mostly poor folks who got swept up in the crack wave because crack was far less expensive and much easier to get than coke. So you had poor people – and if you want to read that as inner-city black folks, then go ahead – being slammed with 30-, 40-, and 50-year sentences for having one little rock of a weekend's escape from the city. While you had your rich people – and if you want to read that as suburban, gated-community white folks, then go ahead – getting off with sentences that were a mere fraction of those given to crack users because they could afford the powder instead of the rock.

Call me a BHL if you must (Bleeding Heart etc.), but imagine being pulled over by the cops for having one too many Bud Lights and getting tossed in the slammer, while down the road Executive Eddie gets only a warning for being tanked on his Chimay Ale. Your lawyer then explains to you if you'd blown .08 on Chimay instead of Bud you wouldn't be in the pokey because of the new Sliding Sloshed Scale Law handed down by Congress.

Or you could liken it to paying $4.19 a gallon to fill up your Pinto instead of $3.59 if only you owned a Porsche or a Ferrari. Or a Beemer, even. I'll give ya one more just for the threesome: It's like being slapped with a five-year sentence for being caught red-handed (and, I guess, red other things) with an ugly hooker as opposed to getting off with a year's probation for being in the company of an elegant, beautiful "escort." "Oh, you're a hooker? I just thought I was doing great with you." Rest in peace, Sir Dudley.

Now, let me circle back. I know the bell rang, but stay right where you are. Again, I neither condone nor condemn. I merely cajole. And sometimes canoodle. And canuck. I'm here merely to point out life's little inequities. Yes, this will be on the test. Yes, it will be multiple choice. All right, all right, get the hell out of here.

# DON'T TAKE YOUR KITCHEN FOR GRANITE

We've been camping out in our own house for weeks now, and I think I'm actually getting the hang of it. You see, my dear wife decided recently it was time to upgrade our kitchen and downstairs guest bathroom, and, like the naïve simpleton I am, I glibly went along with it all.

I presumed this entailed dabbing on a fresh coat or two of paint, getting a new commode cover, and buying a fancy oven mitt or three.

No, sir. "Upgrade" by my wife's definition meant, of course, demolishing all countertops, tearing off all wall coverings, and conducting interviews with no fewer than 59 contractors, handymen, painters, tile folks, grout guys, electrical experts, plumbing people, sink installers, toilet types, granite excavators, countertop wholesalers, and all kinds of strange, hairy men who have been traipsing in and out of our house at all hours doing God only knows what.

So at present our groceries are in little clumps and piles all over the place, and our family forages for food intermittently, pretty much Cro-Magnon style. I keep a stash of chips and cookies hidden in my own special place, just to be safe. Every man for himself, you know.

And for weeks now our humble little abode has taken on the appearance of an archeological dig for ancient artifacts. In fact, amid the dust and debris I was amazed to discover some ancient artifacts of my very own, such as floppy disks from one of my early attempts at the Mediocre American Novel. Floppy disks, mind you. Pre-internet era. Thank God they can only be accessed by now-obsolete technology because I don't want anybody looking at this stuff.

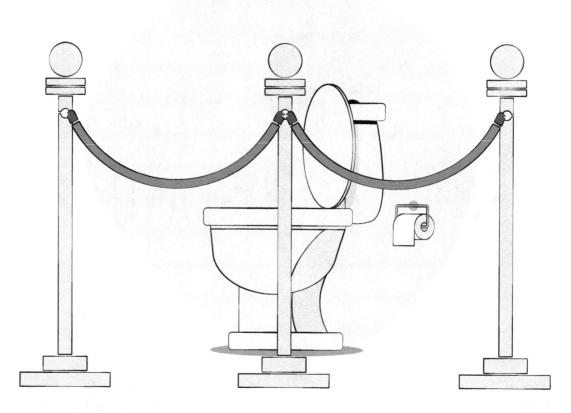

*"Oh, James," Harriet opined, deciding it was better not to tell her former lover that the baby she carried was not his or even his brother's but that of the motorcycle gang leader she hitched a ride with back in Needles, California. Harriet trudged off into the dark and stormy night, not knowing if James would ever want her back or, for that matter, if he'd want her front.*

You get the idea. This is treasure better left buried.

Anyway, through all the smoke and drill bits and extension cords and horrible noise, I do believe something is starting to take shape. Our countertops, which I must admit I never really gave a second thought to, are now a gleaming river of exquisite polished granite. I'm scared to put anything on them now. I don't feel worthy. Our cat's pretty skittish about the whole deal, as well. When he hops up on the countertop, he's at risk of skating freeform all the way across the kitchen and into the dining room. Schweeee..... thunk! Meow?

Moreover, our downstairs bathroom sink has been transformed into this fascinating concave of hammered copper, beautiful and odd. I think of Abe Lincoln every time I wash my hands now. (Y'know, he's on the penny and all.) I feel the need to be very quiet in the downstairs bathroom all of a sudden, I guess because it has taken on this aura of a stately museum. It is gorgeous and finely appointed, and presently I can't do my business in there because I'm a bit intimidated. When I'm in there, I start thinking, "Man, this room doesn't deserve this. I'm should get outta here." I'm of a mind to rope off the downstairs john with velvet and have a docent charge admission.

And through it all, I have become good friends with our main contractor guy, Bruce, who happens to be a Cowboys fan like me. We've practically shared half the season together. I've noticed, however, that I've begun to hope and pray for dull games because if anything really exciting happens while Bruce is tiling our kitchen backsplash, it ain't good. "Touchdown, Cowboys!" Smash, flinkle, kar-rump. "Uh, Mr. White."

I've also become well-versed in the finer points of Contractor Time. You see, there's Eastern Time, Central, Mountain, Pacific—and Contractor Time (CT). When a contractor says he'll be at your house by 8 a.m., that actually means 10:30 a.m. CT. If he says he's heading to lunch for an hour, what he means is he's heading to lunch for three hours and forty-five minutes CT. And, when your friendly contractor guy tells you he can have that job finished in two weeks, this, of course, equates to two and half months CT.

I'm just funnin' ya, Bruce. Ya done good, son. Just remember, no tiling while Romo's in the pocket. And can I take this oxygen mask off now?

# THE JURY'S STILL OUT ON THIS COLUMN. WAY, WAY OUT.

You'll pardon me if I flex my whack-a-lawyer muscles again, but it's not my fault this time. It's true that I swore to my friends of the barrister bent that I would lay off for a while since my last acerbic attorney attack, in which I believe I opined something to the effect of the following:

> "Q: So you're stuck on a desert island with Hitler, a 100-pound rabid wolf, and a lawyer, and you have a gun with only two bullets in it. What do you do?
>
> A: Shoot the lawyer twice."

Rimshot, applause, applause. No, I was going to pen a nice, droll little piece about the agonies of the upcoming Christmas shopping season, mainly pointing out all the unfathomably extraneous must-purchase gift doodads at places like Brookstone—such as those internet-linked patty thermometers that you can insert into your burgers as you grill them to determine not only the very millisecond that the epicenter of your ground beef mound hits optimum ingesting temperature but also to pinpoint and track the temperature of each patty morsel as it works its way through your backyard barbecue guests' digestive systems, just for fun.  This is what I was going to write about. How thoughtless gifts have come a long, mysterious way since the era of maritime-themed tie tacks and microphone-shaped soap on a rope.

Alas, that column was not to be, for again I have been sidetracked, this time by that little letter we all receive from the county clerk now and again that makes us all earnestly yearn for a hefty dose of the chicken pox: the dreaded jury summons.

Yes. So the very day I had set aside to congeal all of my yuletide shopping horror stories into a bouncy little missive for your wonder and amusement was spent instead deep in the bowels of the Travis County Courthouse listening to defense and plaintiff legal beagles grill me and approximately 50 other total strangers on whether or not we could be fair and impartial in this really twisted case of . . . ooh, sorry, I can't divulge that information. Judge's orders, ya know. All I can say about the case is ew, yuck, OMG, and I didn't know such a thing was anatomically possible with a regulation-size bowling pin.

As prospective jurors, we all had to sit through five grueling hours of *voir dire*, which is Latin for "your embarrassing past is now on display to determine if your biased, bigoted, and emotionally disturbed personality precludes you from jury service." The lengths some folks go to avoid their civic duty, I must say, never ceases to amaze. One lady, I kid you not, interrupted the judge no fewer than nine times with such questions as "Is the prosecutor the same thing as the attorney?" By the time this old gal was hustled away, the rest of us weren't sure if it was an act or not, but she was unceremoniously handed a "get out of jury service free" card and awarded six free DVDs of *Judge Judy* Season One. One large man in front of me claimed post-traumatic stress disorder from grievous wounds received during his military service as a means of skipping out, but when pressed by one of the attorneys on the specifics of his war injuries he 'fessed up that he was beaned in the back of the head by a car part in his motorpool job. Yeah, right. Keep your seat, Mr. Purple Heart. I was Prospective Juror #18, and by the time the lawyers took turns whittling away all their undesirables, it appeared that I was seriously headed for ye olde jury box. However, a late question by the defense team saved the day. They asked me what my wife did for a living, and I proudly proclaimed that dear Sue works for, you guessed it, a downtown law firm. "You mean she works with lawyers? Like us?" "Yup." "Do you believe this fact might hinder your ability to render a fair and impartial verdict in this case?" "Uh, probably not. Giggle. Fry 'em." "What did you say?" "Nothing." Then both legal teams hustled to the bench to whisper things back and forth to the judge, and the next thing I knew I was on the street.

Hoohah! I mean, darn. Oh, well. I had fully intended to serve if called upon. I mean, Twelve Angry Men is one of my favorite movies. I wanted to be Henry Fonda, or Lee J. Cobb, or Jack Klugman even. However, I did not emerge unscathed by my brush with our cantankerous court system. When I finally got to my car, I found my windshield papered with a nice collection of parking tickets, courtesy of Austin's finest. Now, that's a good scam. Where's my lawyer?

# LIGHT UP A SMOOTH CHESTERTON'S AND ENJOY THIS COLUMN, WON'T YOU?

Wow. I've been reading lately how these crafty internet marketing types prowl the vast jungle of blog sites on this here World Wide Webby thing to see which sites are getting more and more hits as the days go by. Then they pounce, you see, and offer all kinds of payola and other goodies to the blog hosts to let them advertise on their blog sites. The marketing types' clients are happy because they get more traffic and word of mouth about their fantastic products and services, and the bloggers are happy because they get nifty payola and other goodies simply for referring their loyal readers to these guys who advertise on their sites. And the blog readers are happy, I suppose, because they get what you call "value added" bonus material (this can also be read as obnoxious advertising and teeth-clenching pop-ups) on their favorite blog sites.

The only problem with this scenario is that the integrity of ye olde blog site owner comes into question. Somehow the purity of the message seems tainted when a corporate sponsor gets involved. You start wondering, now, did he write a whole column on how the Nazis were just a misunderstood political faction bent on strict law and order because he really believes it or because the Volkswagen logo is now splashed all over his web page? It's kind of like how every first down the Texas Longhorns make when they're playing at Royal Memorial Stadium is now brought to you by Taco Bell. Not that I'm implying that the makers of Volkswagen are Nazis somehow or that the only reason the 'Horns strive for every hard-earned first down when they're playing at home is because they get a free bag of burritos with every 10 yards. But you get the idea.

So, anyway. Wouldn't you know it? The very day I'm reading about how all this works, I get an e-mail from a guy named Mark Ettingtipe asking me if I would consider pasting some obnoxio—er, I mean, if I would consider developing some mind-nourishing value-added information for my li'l old blog site. How about that? Enough of you crazies have had absolutely nothing better to do than poke around reading my meandering streams of thought so that some crafty marketing types have been prodded to fishing in these waters for an advertising deal. I'm so flattered, you guys. (Insert Sally Field voice here.) "You like me! You really, really like me!"

I have to say, I gave some very serious consideration to the guy's offer. I mean, jeez, an eighth of a cent per reader hit adds up over time. Let's do the math. Say I get approximately 150 reader hits a day, multiplied by my sweet deal of an eighth of a penny per hit, and this comes out to about $1.20 a month. As one Jeff Spicoli once opined in *Fast Times at Ridgemont High*: "Righteous bucks."

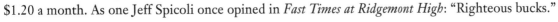

It was a tough call, but I turned ol' crafty Mark Ettingtype down. For one thing, I just can't be untrue to my dear column—and to you, my loyal readers. My mission here is to provide true pearls of wisdom and wit that can only come from a pure heart and a mind influenced only by the odd residual chemicals still left floating in yonder brain canals from my halcyon days of … well, let's just call it "life experimentation" and leave it at that. I still say the color orange has a distinct sound.

And for another thing, I'm not certain I'm quite on board with the products Mr. Ettingtype was wanting to peddle on these here pages. So you'll be glad to know that you won't have to ever wonder about the content on this site at least. They tried, yes sir, but they couldn't get this old soldier to sell out to Madison Avenue. It'll take much more than the lure of some easy money to turn the head of this ol' keyboard banger. But this does remind me—you know what does turn my head? I'll tell you, it's the sweet, luxurious aroma of Chesterton's 100s Menthol-Tipped Cigarettes. Whenever I'm tired from a long day of writing, I like to relax in my favorite easy chair with a cold drink and the silky smooth menthol tobacco flavor of a refreshing Chesterton.

Won't you join me next week when I'll be penning an enjoyable, light-hearted piece of humor about the wacky adventures of visiting the in-laws over Christmas? Pull up a chair, fill your best pipe with Chesterton's nutmeg-aroma pipe tobacco, and we'll share a laugh or two. See you then!

# WHAT IF THURBER NEVER GOT SHOT? AND OTHER PARTY CONVERSATIONS...

Did you know, fellow life travelers, that the wonderful author James Thurber was accidentally shot in the eye with an arrow by his brother while they were playing William Tell as children and so Thurber lost his vision in that eye and that some neurologists think that because Thurber lost vision in that eye that he developed an amazingly creative imagination due to very vivid and complex hallucinations he experienced—hallucinations that are caused by a medical condition called Charles Bonnet syndrome, in which otherwise mentally healthy people suffer wild delusions and lifelike hallucinations due to what researchers believe is the mind's attempt to meld reality and perception into a "forged vision" to make up for the loss of the person's biological vision, which may or may not be, in fact, true and provable; however, it does stand to reason, if the example of one James Thurber is held up as the prototypical Charles Bonnet syndrome sufferer because we all know what extraordinarily unique works Thurber composed, such as *The Secret Life of Walter Mitty* and *The Catbird Seat* and *If Grant Had Been Drinking at Appomattox*, and furthermore this makes you wonder if Thurber had not been shot in the eye by his brother when he was a child, would he not have become one of America's great humorists—which then makes me ponder my own fate because, you see, when I was a tyke, I was quite puny and small and was picked on quite a bit by my larger, more sadistic classmates, and because of such bullying, I believe, I developed an "I'll show you" attitude and was therefore determined to prove that I was just as good, if not better, than my tormentors, which I'm sure is a very common personality factor in many

folks, which is certainly why I drove myself to make all A's in school, graduate valedictorian, run the mile faster than anybody else in a 200-mile radius of my hometown, and this, of course, leads me to further postulate that childhood bullying, accidents, trauma, wedgies, and bedwetting are the likely root causes for much of the world's great works because it is at that delicate stage in a person's emotional development that deep-seeded drives and needs are planted and thus if some snot-nosed kid pushes you down on the playground—and surely he's doing such because his own home life is utterly dysfunctional—then this is something you internalize, perhaps even subconsciously, for years and years until one day, when you are in your late sixties and you realize that all your life you have pushed the limits and crossed the boundaries and explored the heights and depths of your soul because some stupid little asswipe knocked your books out of your hand, and it is at this moment that you pause and reflect and think, wait a minute, you're saying that everything I've achieved up to this moment in time I owe to Thomas Bedford and his gang of thugs, and then you take another drink and come to your senses and everything falls back into place and your arms and legs slowly reattach themselves to you and you float gently down into the chair that you suddenly remember you were sitting in and you realize you are at a New Year's Eve party in the neighborhood and you've been chatting with some couple from two blocks over and you can't remember their names and it's just as well anyway because they wandered off to talk to other people when you started getting that glazed look in your eye and began to exhibit early symptoms of catatonia, but then the party hostess comes over and smiles and give you a couple of pigs in blankets, which you greedily devour and realize, whew, it's about time to go home.

# THE NITROUS
# BEFORE CHRISTMAS

'Twas the week before Christmas, and into my face
I stuffed all sorts of candies, cookies, and delectibles saccharase.

The fillings of my molars were hard-pressed to hold firm,
And sure enough one crumbled, oh, how I did squirm.

A frantic call to the dentist, dear ol' Doctor Devry,
Set the rescue in motion, oh, why, Doctor, why?

So the doc with her toolkit filled me kindly with gas
For hours full of grinding, what a pain in the ass.

While high on the nitrous, why, what should appear,
But Santa and his elves and nine purple reindeer.

Away to the rinse basin I flew like a flash
To tell doc of this miracle, this was better than hash!

As I rinsed and I spat, Santa called them by name,
On Jimi, on Janis, on Jerry, and whatshisname,

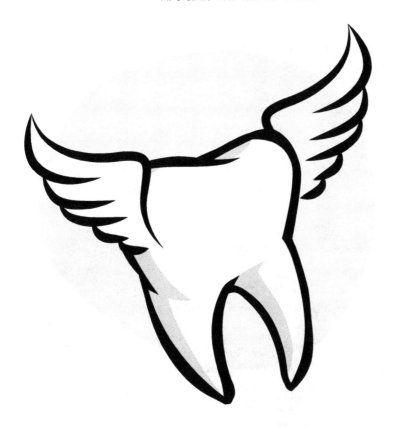

To the top of the room! To the top of the office!
When the nitrous wears off, he may try to off us!

As round Frisbees before the concert fly
When meet with an officer mount for the sky,

So up through the HVAC system they flew,
Santa and his rockin' reindeer and Jerry Lee, too.

And then in a twinkling I heard on the ceiling,
A prancing and pawing, or maybe my brain was peeling,

As I drew in my head and was turning around,
Doc Devry came with more gas, whoopee, another round!

She was dressed all in fur or maybe it was double-knit,
Man, this nitrous was some really good sh*t.

A bundle of tools she had in each hand,
Hell, I didn't care, I was feeling mighty grand.

Her eyes how they twinkled, she was enjoying this parade!
Dentists must study at the School of Marquis de Sade.

My droll little mouth by now was quite numb
Even while she made mincemeat of my teeth and my gums.

The beard of her chin was as white as the snow,
Wait, that's her mask, ooh, look how it glows.

The light on her head looked alien in a way,
Or somehow transcendent like Faye Dunaway.

She had a broad face and she pressed on my belly
To get a better angle at her grinding so smelly.

She was chubby and plump, or maybe it was the gas,
'cause now she had three eyes and smelled like sassafras.

I laughed as she drilled in spite of myself,
Then I saw all her books melt off the shelf.

A wink of her eye and a 360 twist of her head
Made me realize this was best left unsaid.

She spoke not a word but kept straight at her work,
While I counted the rhinos and tried not to jerk.

And laying her finger aside of my nose,
She said stop sucking on the vacuum hose.

Then she sprang from the chair, to her assistant gave a whistle,
"Help Mr. White," said she. "He's ready for dismissal."

But I heard her exclaim as she put away her drill,
"You feel happy now, wait'll you get my bill."

# LET'S TALK ABOUT KEITH. AND TEETH. AND SIR EDWARD HEATH.

**M**y reading list of late, aside from the requisite comics and sports sections, has included *Life*, the autobiography of Rolling Stones guitarist Keith Richards, or Keef as most of you know him. It is a fascinating read, I must say, not simply because you get to peek behind the heroin- and cocaine-caked curtain of Sir Keef's life and gain a foothold of understanding of how this supremely talented Brit bluesman/rock icon with the biological resilience of mutant cockroach has managed to stay alive lo these many years, but you also get a marvelously witty insight into the keen and strangely aloof mind of a songwriter — what makes him tick, what amazingly broad array of cues he picks up on as inspiration for his songs, the unbelievably rich life he's led (from stealing and reselling used bottles to scrape enough money together to eat to jetting from Morocco to the south of France with the world's most beautiful and exotic people), and his wonderfully unique take on life and how he's riffed through it plucking those nasty, jangly rhythms with nary a scratch despite spending more than 50 years on the hard edge of a lifestyle that has taken down many a talented man and woman long before their time.

Some have called the Stones "the world's most dangerous rock and roll band" in their prime, and if they were, then Sir Keef was the man wielding the blade. A dear friend of mine lent me the book, and going in I thought, yah, another ghostwritten alcohol-slopped tell-all with some deftly dropped names and a few juicy "gotcha" moments with just enough backstory on some of the Stones' most famous numbers

and people and hangers-on to keep me reading. Man, was I wrong. Richards can tell tales. And his insight into musical concepts, history, and how circumstance, events, and people being in certain places at certain times caused modern popular music to evolve as it has is quite remarkable. So, do I recommend picking up this book? Hell, yes. And there are many photos. Later on we'll get ice cream.

Anyway, all this to say, wow, I far underestimated Sir Keef's literary acumen; however, in retrospect, I shouldn't have been surprised. I have always stood (sometimes sat, depending on the subject and my current blood pressure) in slight awe of most things British. I mean, Richards may or may not be smarter than your average rock guitarist, but a little voice inside me tells me his British upbringing brings a little to bear. I mean, think about it. British musicians basically took American rock and stepped it up to a higher, thinking man's level, didn't they? Most of the best, most progressive rock outfits in history come from our tiny mother country: The Beatles, The Stones, Led Zeppelin, Yes, The Moody Blues, The Who, The Yardbirds, The Zombies, King Crimson, Pink Floyd, Procol Harum, ELP — need I go on?

The same goes for comedy. The Brit sense of humor has always struck me as two beats faster, more subtle, and exquisitely more wry than that of the comics on this side of the pond. Don't get me wrong; I love Steve Martin, Richard Pryor, Stephen Wright, and all the others as much as the next guy, but when it comes to writing, content, delivery, and timing, no one tops the Brits in my book. Monty Python, Fawlty Towers, Dudley Moore with Sir John Gielgud in "Arthur" – to me, that's comedic nirvana. I know that some of you don't get Monty Python. I also know that you are the people who faithfully attend NASCAR events, wear camouflage vests to restaurants, and worship at the altar of Larry the Cable Guy and Jeff Foxworthy. That's OK. I have no problem with that. (I can just hear the crayons hitting the paper now: "If'n yew love them faggoty Brits so much then why don't yew git on outta here and move over thar then. That's rite, jus take the bus on over thar, ya dam trater.")

Anyway, where were we? Ah, humor, music, insight. All that. I guess the only thing I can't understand about our dear British comrades, being that they are so refined and intelligent and talented, is the thing with their teeth. With everything the mighty British Empire has achieved through the ages, you would think they would have caught on to the whole dental hygiene kick by now. I mean, gads. I guess the followers of Larry the Cable Guy and our Union Jack cousins do have something in common: a somewhat laissez-faire attitude on ye olde oral health.

Criminy. How I got off on teeth and NASCAR is beyond me, but if you do happen upon Keith Richards' book, by all means…. Now, where'd I leave my floss?

# MORE LENTICULAR HAIKU, BY SIR ARCHIE FERNDOODLE

Fellow time/space voyagers and other occasional devotees of "This Old Blouse," I am more tickled than a duffel bag full of marsupials to announce the return of my dear friend, front porch sartorial mentor, and fellow breakfast-nook philologist, Sir Archie Ferndoodle (applause, applause, applause).

Yes, the former poet laureate of the Greater Southwestern Scribes Society, which meets every third Thursday in the back of Sue's Salon in Cement, Texas, has been gently coaxed out of quasi-retirement to once again bless us with phrasings, words, syllables, parts of syllables, and renderings of nocturnal animal sounds from the Ulan Bator region as only Sir Archie can. (And remember, if you mention this column at Sue's Salon, you get 10 percent off a five-ounce jar of Sue's Coconut Heel Scrub with the purchase of at least $20, not including her patented Tomato-Lye Jamboree Hair Tonic.)

As I'm sure you remember, the esteemed Fernie holds an associate's degree in postmodern comparative limerick studies from the University of Southern Panama's Correspondence College and has been featured five times in the *American Anthology of Poetry*. Just a few of his classics include "Oh, Staff Sergeant, My Staff Sergeant!," "Why Is the Man Always from Nantucket?," "The Squirrels Stopped Talking to Me Today," and his latest, "A Stitch, a Horse, and a Can of Pearl," which was the inside-cover poem in the most recent edition of the *Cement Area Greensheet*.

The more astute of you may have seen Fernie's hand in the Christmas edition of "This Old Mouse." Raise your hand if you had the notion that Sir Archie was the ghostpen behind "The Nitrous Before Christmas." Well, you're dead wrong; I wrote that while flying low in my dentist's office, but I did have ol' Fernie in mind. In fact, he may have actually inhabited my body during that whole experience, but we digress again.

So anyway, without further magoo, I give you Sir Archie Ferndoodle, who has just returned from a five-month sojourn at the Tao Sendaha Haiku Sweat Lodge, just north of Pittsburgh.

### Lenticular Haiku
*by Archie Ferndoodle*

Hand old, withered
Extended to young happy boy who
Smiles and
Coughs up a small border town near
Flagstaff.

Deposit slip with no meaning flutters
In brown surge of empty day. I find Julia at
Home making love to the Buick
Again.
Better judgment whispered
Toyota, Toyota.
Toyota. Smash hindsight with
Bitter hammer of stoli rocks. Ah.

Three grateful invertebrates argue
On who passed
Wind while each ascends
The assistant professor's
Mortgage.

Trees and earth know much more
Than they sing
To man accused of listening of listening
Of listening to Alex
Trebek and his minions. Only refuse
And then hear again, the daily
Double. Oh! Bodies of
Water for Four
Hundred.

Heat. No heat. Heat. No heat.
Damn toaster. Fling the
Shiny monster down the hillock to
CRASH waves of filament element
Parchment and wire. No heat toast is mere
bread and
Sorrow.
Dear Julia. I'm trading it
In.

# FOLLOW YOUR DREAMS? WELL, OK, BUT HAVE A BACKUP PLAN

*Author's note: For you dedicated, sort of dedicated, and even not-so-dedicated followers of TOS, I feel I must warn you in advance. This particular installment lacks any juvenile silliness, nonsensical babble, slice-of-life inanity, random wordplay, serpentine stream of consciousness, thinly veiled parody, and/or incomprehensible doublespeak. I'm actually taking a stab at being serious this time. This likely won't last long, as most of my prescriptions seem to have run out.*

As I watch my daughters grow into young womanhood—Lindsey now a thoughtful, creative high school sophomore so marvelously free-spirited yet touchingly conscientious in every facet; and Jamie, our firebrand eighth-grader so fiercely strong-willed and stubborn but so tender-hearted and self-conscious—I struggle to keep them optimistic and open to the great vista of opportunities and adventures that is theirs in their youth while ensuring that they truly understand the many gambles attendant with life's every turn.

How do you convey to your children that life is to be thoroughly enjoyed yet doggedly pursued with utmost seriousness, that the world around them is not a vile place to be feared but that wariness and caution are also fundamental?

How do you keep those most precious to you warm-hearted and open to the world when, while you're teaching your oldest how to drive a car, a man pulls up next to her and flips her the finger because she's driving too slow for his taste? What course do you take when your youngest tells you that some anony-

mous degenerate claiming to be an online friend wrote such depraved and loathsome things on her web page that the words don't even bear repeating?

Beyond these random acts of unkindness, how do you also instill in your children the passion to "follow your dreams"—a catchphrase heard so often in movies, media, books, commercials, speeches, campaign promises, and valedictory addresses today that it has become hackneyed and meaningless—when the cold reality is that the vast majority of us grinding out our day-to-day existences have come nowhere near the lofty dreams of our youth?

Don't get me wrong; I'm not saying that anyone should settle for something less than what one earnestly wants to do with one's career and life. I'm merely advocating, in this reality-TV culture that falsely suggests that everyone can be a star, for a healthy dose of practicality. I fear that many kids growing up today, buffeted from all sides by messages insinuating that instant fame or fortune will be theirs for the taking when some magic day arrives, will be in for a terribly rude awakening when it comes time to settle into that desk job in the corporate cubicle farm.

A glimpse at one episode of "American Idol" confirms this unsettling notion. When the judges break the bitter truth to so many young would-be superstars who can't carry a tune in a large fruit bowl, the contestants' reaction of utter disbelief and heartbreak may make for a sort of Schadenfreudean entertainment for the masses, but it also exposes symptoms of delusional expectations held by today's youth. Yeah, you're going to win the 750-million-to-1-shot lottery with one ticket. Right.

Ah, hell, I guess it's not just today's youth. I'll fess up. When I was 11, and I caught my first touchdown pass of the season for the Burleson Boys Club Panthers, I was immediately convinced I would be an NFL wide receiver. That touchdown was the only pass I ever caught that season—and for the rest of my football career (which lasted until eighth grade when I broke my collarbone). A high schooler who weighs all of 130 pounds sopping wet stands little chance at football glory outside of his back yard.

When I was 14, I was going to be a drummer in a rock band that would be discovered by a West Coast record label and shoot straight to international stardom. Talent seemed to be the snag here (see "American Idol" above). When I was 19, I was going to own my own legion of vending machines, which held the promise of easy riches and an unending supply of M&Ms, but no one seemed to want to lend a teenage entrepreneur the mere six figures for start-up.

And when I was 30-something and finished my first attempt at the Mediocre American Novel, I was sure I was destined to be the next John Irving. Alas, that dream is still on the runway, desperately awaiting clearance in the thickening fog. So I soldier on, in the cube farm, telling myself that John Irving probably doesn't really have it that good.

And I also tell my girls, yes, follow your dreams—but have a solid backup plan. If you truly want to be the next Lady Gaga, give it a shot. But stay on course for your MBA, as well. Please.

# LIFE, DEATH, AND THE IMPORTANCE OF THE HYPHEN

**P**ardon me while I slowly lose my mind.

You've heard of the axiom regarding higher learning: It's the pursuit of learning more and more about less and less until you know absolutely everything about nothing. It's an ivory tower conundrum. Academic types, in the never-ending quest to gain all the knowledge they can on a particular subject—say, the reproduction rituals of the sub-Saharan aardvark—eventually become self-professed experts in this one tiny field of endeavor, often to a maddening nth degree and to the exclusion of everything else, including, sadly, common sense.

You've witnessed this.

You at cocktail party: "So you're a professor?"

Academic type: "I'm a Ph.D., yes. Also Ed.D., M.e.D., M.B. B., B.B.S., and M.Ou.S.E. By the way, did you know that the anal glands of the bushland aardvark actually lure members of the opposite sex? I have photos."

You: "Oh, look at the time."

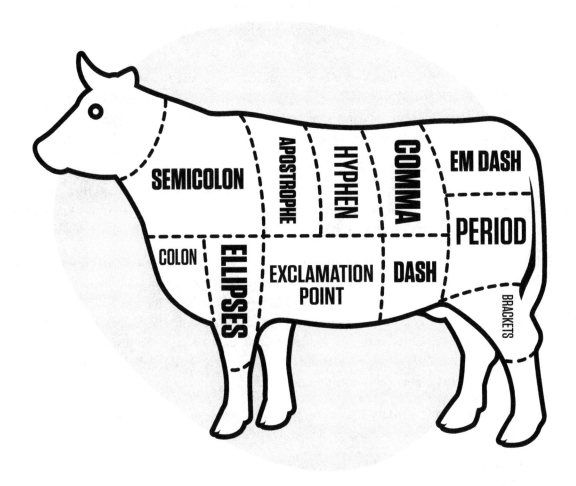

Graphically, this phenomenon can be represented as a triangle with a nice, fat base at the bottom and a teensy-weensy point at the top that goes infinitely on up into nothingness. Poof! Gone. Bye bye!

This gives me a mental image of a vanishing point, which stirs my addled mind to remember the movie *Vanishing Point*, in which a guy named Kowalski is hired to deliver a 1970 Dodge Challenger to another guy in San Francisco, who bets Kowalski that he can't get the car from Colorado to California in less than 15 hours. It's a nice cult movie from the '70s, and you should rent it, but I don't know why I'm mentioning it now.

Um. Where were we? Ah, yes. Here's what I'm getting at. My own, little personal ivory tower hell, which is currently gnawing my intestines into mush, is all about words. You see, I work as an editor in a quasi-large association here in association land (don't get me started), and I work with other editor types in this whisper-quiet stable crammed with dozens of little, square cubicles. I feel like one of those cows they raise for veal. Just sitting here. All day. Clacking away. Waiting for the eventual slaughter. Moo. Clack. Sip. Burp. Moo. Clack. Lunch! Moo. Clack. Sip. Burp.

Anyway, after oh, about 25 years of doing this, my daily goal has become simply this: do my job, write my stories, drink my 18 cups of coffee, moo, try to make as little fuss as possible, and oh, so thankfully go home. But it doesn't work that way. Moo.

We have to have meetings. About things such as the hyphen. And we have to have meetings about having meetings about the hyphen. When should we use the hyphen? Will there be trouble if the hyphen is misused in this instance? Should we establish a hyphen resource center? What size hyphen should we use? What if we run out of hyphens? Is there a proper hyphen font?

You get my drift. I suppose I should be more passionate about my craft. Don't get me wrong, I consider myself a pretty decent writer/editor, and I think I do my job well, but some of the things that stir up the dust around here are making my left eyelid twitch. It could be the java, but I don't think so. I mean, who besides the editor types sitting around me really cares if "decision making" is hyphenated or not? Moo!

It's not that I don't care, but as a now-deceased colleague once opined, "I've seen life and death, and this ain't it." This guy was once the executive director of my quasi-large association, and a wise man he was. His many life experiences included a military stint in Vietnam, so I embrace his take on the big picture—which is basically this: The fervent dispute that's twisting your innards into salt-water taffy usually doesn't really mean that much in the larger scope of things, so relax. I know from whence I speak, as well. I was an air traffic controller long ago, before my venture into the world of words, and it's true—hundreds of people won't die if we can't come to agreement on this hyphen.

I'm sure people in other professions have the same problem. Passionate arguments, dust-ups, and angry looks arise from what in reality is the tiniest minutiae. You want to scream "Get a life! Please. Moo!"

But you don't. You nod, you agree to the latest treatise on the hyphen, which becomes Association Communications Policy Number A-165, and you quietly pray for a stray meteor. Ah, well. At least I have my health. Ooh, what is that rash on my…

# RECONNAISSANCE SPECIALIST ZORBUM 9SMITH REPORTS

"Oh, I used to be disgusted,
And now I try to be amused…"
—*Elvis Costello*

"Irony can be pretty ironic sometimes."
—*Commander Buck Murdock, Airplane II, The Sequel*

Floating far above the clouds somewhere over the Great Plains, a gargantuan monolithic door composed of a mysterious synthetic skin slides silently up, and the great silver mothership swallows a lozenge-shaped shuttlecraft.

Reconnaissance Specialist Zorbum 9Smith exits the shuttlecraft and immediately reports to Captain Vnnn-pu. After the traditional Andromedan earlobe-sniffing ceremony of greeting, Specialist 9Smith readies for the debriefing.

"9Smith," Captain Vnnn-pu mindmelds, "your mission was to observe this planet's most advanced, most powerful nation and report on your impressions of its culture. What are your findings?"

"Honored Captain, if you would open your mind to Subchannel Y, I have prepared a Mental Power-Point presentation," 9Smith melds. "I believe you will be most intrigued, as was I. Please disregard those first two slides. That is me at a ritualistic labor ceremony of the Western world."

"What is this ritualistic labor ceremony called?"

"The happy hour," 9Smith reports. "Work force representatives convene at small, local shrines to partake of what I can only presume are holy elixirs, plot overthrow of their labor overlords, and perform pre-mating functions with work force representatives of the opposite sex."

"I see. The gyrations are quite peculiar. And what is that device on your subcranium?"

"That is termed a lamp shade," 9Smith melds, referring to his notes. "Apparently, this is a sacred crown worn during the advanced stages of the happy hour ceremony."

"Good." Captain Vnnn-pu nods, mentally smiling. "You must have gained their trust to be honored so. And your report?"

"This is a land of many ironies, Captain. And I know how a good irony sets your drachio-chords to vibrating."

"Yes, yes. Juicy irony."

"Observe your mindscreen, Captain. These are just a few examples:

"In this culture, personal vehicles that would save the most currency for drivers—electric vehicles the earthlings have finally invented to run without using deceased dinosaur fluids—are priced out of reach for those drivers who would need the currency savings the most."

"Most odd," Captain Vnnn-pu notes.

"It becomes worse," 9Smith melds. "Domestic energy alternatives, such as solar panels, energy-efficient windows and doors, and appliances that cost the least currency to operate—and even longer-lasting, currency-saving light-producing modules—are the very things the poor among this society cannot afford."

Captain Vnnn-pu mentally sighs. "Continue."

"It seems that humans who operate their personal vehicles the fastest on earth streets and highways are generally the humans least qualified to drive at any speed."

"Hmm."

"Further, the media with the most power to influence humans in this culture—movies and television—and would therefore obviously hold themselves to the highest standards of storytelling, worthwhile entertainment, and adherence to the principle of doing the most good for the most people, instead regularly produce such products as 'Booty Call,' 'Dude, Where's My Car?', 'Keeping Up with the Kardashians,' and 'The Jerry Springer Show,' to name just a few."

Captain Vnnn-pu shudders, his drachio-chords humming.

"Also, professions that have the potential to make the most positive impact on cultural progress—such as teaching—are consistently near the bottom of the human pay scale, while those who play children's games for a living make millions of earth dollars per year."

"Astounding."

"What's more, these fully grown children-men are idolized and revered by most everyone in the society—namely the males—despite the children-men's propensity to disregard the society's laws and morés, injure their spouses and themselves with firearms, ingest illegal performance-enhancing substances, and generally behave like preteen humans."

"I must sit," Captain Vnnn-pu admits. "My drachio-chords. Go on."

"Those humans with the most varied and abundant life experiences, who would be revered and honored by any thinking society—the elderly—are by and large relegated to the shadows, often to die alone, in poverty, or in dormitory-like detention centers known as care facilities.

"And get this, the humans who vie for public office are most interesting. These humans claim to have 'the average Joe's values at heart,' yet they are generally among the most very wealthy and privileged among them. From my observation, the average human citizen wouldn't have anywhere near the financial means, the family pedigree, the television actor's visage, or the innate ability to switch sentiments on a whim as do these humans. A most perplexing and frightening breed."

"Who are these humans?"

"They call them politicians, Captain. A most untrustworthy type, yet the humans bestow upon them the most power of all, it seems."

"And this 'average Joe?'"

Specialist 9Smith mentally shakes his subcranium. "Apparently, not the brightest of creatures."

"Please, the drachio-chords."

"Lieutenant Kranki-5, please get the captain a container of neep juice."

"Is there more?"

"Oh, much, much more, Captain. I will relate only a few, however. This one possibly intrigues me the most. The very nature of accruing wealth is quite obviously tipped in the favor of the already-wealthy humans."

"What is wealth again, 9Smith?"

"The accumulation of personal currency. Unlike Andromeda, sir, where every citizen is guaranteed equal access to life necessities, here one must earn and trade currency to ensure continued sustenance, care, and shelter."

"Most curious."

"It is a true subcranium-scratcher: The cycle of wealth begetting wealth and poverty begetting poverty appears solid and unshakeable. For the large part, it appears the wealthy human tribes will always be the wealthy, and the same with the poor humans. Any real attempt at wealth-sharing appears lacking."

"Strange. Proceed."

"More is known now among humans about health and nutrition for young humans, and more affordable access to quality choices for human children is available to more families than at any other time in human history, yet childhood obesity and diabetes appear to be at epidemic proportions—and human childhood hunger remains a problem."

"I feel tear duct activation coming on," the captain mutters.

"Additionally, with the advent of cable and satellite, humans now have thousands of television wavelengths available for viewing every night, yet when one mindmelds with the humans, it appears the choices of quality programs are nowhere near as desirable as, say, A.D. 1962—when one could choose from among "The Andy Griffith Show," "The Dick Van Dyke Show," "Gunsmoke," or "The Ed Sullivan Show" from among the three network channels the humans had then."

"Andy Griffith. Was he a great leader?"

"On the local level, yes, Captain. Apparently an outstanding officer of the law."

"Please, no more, 9Smith, no more. Anything positive to report?"

"Well, yes. One of the culture's leaders here announced that humans may soon be able to keep their shoes on when they arrive at air travel centers."

"Shoes?" Captain Vnnn-pu queries. "Why would the humans need to take off their shoes at air travel centers in the first place?"

"It's a long story, Captain."

# WELCOME TO THE ER, 21ST CENTURY STYLE

I get nervous simply approaching the building. The bright lights, the important sounds of rushing people and vehicles—the very feel of emergencies in progress—unsettle my stomach and quicken my pulse.

The evening air is cool, excited by gusts and breezes swirling from the north. A front is moving in, but circumstances give me the impression that even the night is stirred by these critical moments. I'm suddenly covered in goose bumps as I usher my wife and daughter into the reception area.

We accompany our daughter to sign in, and it's obvious from first glance that our situation is not nearly as serious as some of those around us. We are only a minor emergency, so we'll have to wait.

The waiting is interminable. Our daughter bravely holds back the tears.

"It happened to me, too, honey," my wife says, putting a reassuring hand on our daughter's shoulder. "Don't worry. They'll fix it up."

Inside the inner sanctum now, the hushed urgency of myriad conversations and vital tone of learned, caring consult and somber consideration of options and ramifications, mixed with a few cries of desperate pleading against the inevitable, impress upon me that I am without a doubt in a place where decisions, skills, timing, and training mean everything.

We comfort our daughter in the interim, soothing her, trying our best to let her know that everything will be all right. Most of the conversations around us we can't help but hear, picked up only in snippets and instances of outburst and intervals of silence.

"Tell me again what happened exactly."

"He fell, and something just cracked…"

"This is pretty bad."

One solemn couple in the corner is told frankly that there was nothing that could be done. They are escorted into another room. My wife and I exchange glances, slowly shaking our heads.

"Dad…" my daughter begins.

"It's OK, honey, it's not as bad as it looks. I'm sure it's going to be just fine."

One man ahead of us reacts angrily to his diagnosis. He doesn't seem to care who hears him.

"This can't be! There's no way to fix it?!"

"I'm sorry, sir, there's just too much damage."

And finally it's our turn.

"What happened here?"

Our daughter is too caught up in her emotions to speak, so I do it for her.

"She…dropped her baby."

"I see."

Our daughter holds out her shattered, lifeless iPhone, its little face disfigured into a spider web of cracks.

"You can repair that, right?" I ask, suggesting with my optimistic expression that all is well.

"Unfortunately, no, sir. When the screen is cracked like this, there's really nothing you can do."

"It was so young," I offer, gazing wistfully at the dead doohickey.

"It's a phone, dear," my wife says flatly, and I'm suddenly pulled out of my living analogy.

You think I'm joking, you who haven't dropped your baby yet. Just you wait. The Sprint Store (or insert your brand here store) is the new ER, the trauma center of the New Age. Specialists and technicians here are the new doctors and surgeons, making life-and-death decisions on your dropped, drowned, squashed, mashed, or chicken-fried doodad. It's serious business.

I thought my daughter was going to suffer a nervous breakdown while we waited the—oh, God, three days!!—for the replacement doohickey to arrive.

I will admit, I eventually did get a cell phone myself, at my wife's insistence. But I use it as a phone. Imagine that? I have never texted. I don't know how to text, and if it rings while I'm driving, I just let it rumble away in my pants. There is some satisfaction in that.

It is beyond me, and will likely remain far beyond me until I'm a dead doohickey myself, how our kids live and breathe life through their iPhones. I was at a concert not long ago, and I actually saw a girl in the audience watching the concert on her doodad, streaming on the internet. You following me here? The band is RIGHT THERE, live and in spitting distance—and she's looking down at her doodad!

I was tempted to pluck the foul thing from her hands and stomp it into the ground. But then I would have had to accompany her to the ER and start the process all over again.

"What happened here?"

"I squashed her baby."

"I see…"

# AN INSIDER'S PEEK
# AT HOLLYWOOD, PART II

I suppose I had my one real insider's look at how Hollywood works some years ago, when I attended a screenwriters' session on how to "pitch ideas" to producers during an Austin Film Festival annual gathering of would-be writers.

A panel of so-called idea people (a Hollywood oxymoron if I ever heard one) sat at a table and critiqued writers' script ideas, based on approximately 30 seconds of monologue. If writers didn't have what the idea people called a high-concept proposal, if writers paused for a breath, if writers tried to explain a complex plot turn, they were toast.

The guy who won the pitch contest did so with the following idea, I kid you not:

> "So you're walking along the street, a nice sunny day, and suddenly everything goes blank. Then you're like HOLY F@#K!! WHERE AM I?!"

> "Ooh," said the idea people. "Nice."

Cursing and yelling seemed to be high on their list. "High concept," to these folks, who I must say all looked to be about 25 to 28 years old, meant explosions, terror, betrayal, deadly animals, killer robots, slasher horror, or Brad Pitt. This particular pitch session occurred as the movie "Snakes on a Plane" was in production. One of the idea people could hardly contain himself as he explained what a fantastic high-concept film this was going to be—a classic in the making.

"Imagine it," he gushed. "Snakes set loose on a plane! Don't you see? There's no way off of a plane. And all these snakes are slithering all over the place!"

I sat and wondered how this expert panel would have rated the opening scene to the 1951 epic "A Place in the Sun," in which Montgomery Clift is quietly thumbing for a ride along a lonely stretch of road. It was then and there I realized I would never be a Hollywood screenwriter. No, not sour grapes. I'm just not young and stupid enough.

Am I alone here? With very few notable exceptions, this is the state of film-making today. If it bites, blows up, bleeds, beheads people, or is Brad, it's got a green light. If we run out of ideas, we do it all over again as a sequel.

Even my kids, teenage movie buffs both of them, understand by now the banal, bottom-line instincts of your basic Hollywood producer. Both my daughters are big "Twilight Saga" fans, but even they balked at the notion of "The Twilight Saga: Breaking Wind—Part II."

Did I say "Wind"? I meant "Dawn," of course. This latest gem, which opens in November, is a part two *within a multi-part series* of movies, mind you, all of which are looking more and more like the same vampire movie with simply fresh blood and longer fangs.

This got me thinking again. What if the great citizenry—that's us—rose up and dictated to Hollywood: No More Sequels! I know, I know what you're going to say, what about "Godfather II"? Simple, this is the exception that proves the rule. Just about every other sequel I can think of never should have seen the light of day. Here are just a few: "Basic Instinct 2," "Caddyshack II," "Grease 2," "Jaws: The Revenge," "Dirty Dancing: Havana Nights," "Dumb and Dumberer," "Blues Brothers 2000." The list is damn near eternal.

I shudder to think of the results if such movie-making titans as director Stuart Rosenberg ("Cool Hand Luke") or Robert Mulligan ("To Kill a Mockingbird") had been under similar pressure to squeeze out sequels. Oh, the horror.

Come to think of it, there's no time limit on butchering classics. They have a new "Three Stooges" now, for crying out loud. So, as much as it strikes terror in my heart, you might look for these titles soon at a theater near you:

- "Cooler Hand Luke: Revenge of Them Damned Eggs"

- "To Sir With Even More Love"

- "Citizen Kane II: Rosebud Returns"

- "The Ten Commandments II: God's Revisions"

- "Real Gone with the Wind"

- "Bonnie and Clyde Part 2: They Were Only Flesh Wounds"

- "The Post-Graduate: Revenge of the Robinsons"

- "Mockingbird II: Rise of Boo Radley"

- "Dueling Wizards of Oz: I'll Witch-Slap You"

# FOOTBALL TONIGHT: URSINE MAMMALS VS. MIDPRICED SEDANS. HOO AH!

This here story, which you may have heard about already, falls squarely under the "you gotta be kiddin' me" category, because when I read it, I said, "What the f— … er, you gotta be kiddin' me." Yeah, that's what I said.

Here 'tis, and I quote:

"A Utah school district has decided against using Cougars as a mascot for a new high school in part because of the negative connotation of the word in popular culture. Canyons School District Superintendent David S. Doty said the selection of Chargers as the school's mascot was driven by the desire for originality, despite a poll of some future students that showed 26 percent in favor of using the Cougar mascot.

"Doty said that although Brigham Young University, as well as several Utah high schools (including one in a nearby district), use Cougars as a mascot, public comments they received reflect a desire to be different—and he noted that some see the word 'cougar' as carrying a 'negative double entendre.' Spokeswoman Jennifer Toomer-Cook said the power of social media has brought the district more attention than desired, referring to articles like this *Huffington Post* story, 'Cougar Mascot Vetoed for Corner Canyon High School for Being Offensive toward Women,' or this Yahoo sports story, 'New

School Can't Be Cougars Because Middle-Aged Women Might Be Offended.'" Or this here social media story that I'm about to write. Har. Woah, hey, I'm actually writing it right now. AAH! One of those space-time continuum moments. How can I be writing it now if you're already reading it? Hello! hello! Echo! echo! Scary.

So anyway, yeah, all ol' Superintendent Doty had to say was that the school wanted to be different. By bringing up the negative double entendre thing, he opened himself up a big ol' can o' media worms. I like that. Media worms. Kinda fits.

This, of course, got me thinking about what other teams might have to re-ponder their mascot choices, given today's milieu of ultra-hyper-crikey-sensitivity. Let us ponder. And re-ponder. Take the NFL (please):

- *Chicago Bears.* Sorry, gay connotation. If you are unaware, a "bear" in the gay world, and I quote from a popular social media source, refers to male individuals who possess physical attributes much like a bear, such as a heavy build, abundant body hair, and often facial hair. Not that there's anything wrong with that. But, lest we offend our hairy homosexual brethren, let's change it to the **Chicago Ursine Mammals**.

- *Buffalo Bills.* Mmm, negative emotional impact on the financially strapped in our society. Bills, bills, bills. We can't have that. This needs to be something gentler, something along the lines of **Buffalo Payment Restructuring Reminders**.

- *New York Jets.* Nope; this offends those of us who can't afford to fly. From now on, you are the **New York Midpriced Sedans**.

- *New England Patriots.* This is borderline, but I see possible political overtones here. Just to be on the safe side, let's go with the **New England Citizens of No Political Affiliation**.

- *Washington Redskins.* This one's obvious—and the actual name change is already in the works. But instead of Washington Football Team, how about **Washington Human Race Members**. (Same with the Kansas City Chiefs. Come on, fellahs, that's just rude. From here one out, the **Kansas City Regular Decent People of Vague Ethnic Persuasion**.)

- *Tennessee Titans.* Sorry, too reflective of the Titan Missiles, the Space Race, the Cold War, Kruschchev, shoe-pounding and all that. Your new name is the **Tennessee World Peace Initiative**.

- *Oakland Raiders.* Please, this conjures up images of thieves and thugs and other ne'er-do-wells. Try on the **Bay Area Working-Class Magnanimous Helper Types**.

- *Cleveland Browns.* This is downright color elitist. You will from here on take the field as the **Cleveland All-Inclusive Hues**. The helmet, of course, will be white but will change color depending on ambient temperature.

- *Philadelphia Eagles.* Mmmm, too nationalistic. I like the **Philadelphia Countries in Harmony**.

- *New York Giants.* Honestly, this is simply humiliating to short people. The Big Apple's team should now and forever be the **New York Average-Height Folks**. And scratch the Big in front of Apple, while you're at it. Let's just say The Apple. Well, now, wait—that also discriminates, doesn't it? The Fruit. There you go. New York the city its own self is now known as The Fruit.

- *New Orleans Saints.* Really, way too pious and religiously selective. See if this fits: **The New Orleans Non-Proselytizing Spiritually Uplifted Cadre**.

# SIR ARCHIE'S 'WORDS FOR THE NOW'

All right, gang, I'm at a bit of a crossroads here. Don't get me wrong. I'm as big a fan of poet Archie Ferndoodle as anyone, and I consider it an honor to present his unique musings in this forum. But ever since his mom passed away in February at the tender age of 109 (breast implant surgery complications, the poor dear), Sir Archie has taken it upon himself to live with me and my family. Mr. F has seven cats and a dyspeptic parrot that sings '70s country songs in the dead middle of the night. If you've ever been awakened at 2 a.m. to the strangled strains of "Harper Valley PTA," you may have an idea of the trauma. And that's not the worst part. Apparently, Archie is on a strict diet consisting chiefly of pan-fried liver, steamed cabbage, large-curd cottage cheese, and Oreos (with double stuffing). The whole house smells like a marathon gastric bypass surgical procedure.

The wife and kids are calling for drastic action. But I can't put the guy on the street, can I? He's a living legend. In fact, just this morning as we were tidying up after Roscoe the Parrot's . . . uh, indiscretions on my wife's oriental rug, the Great One handed me his latest. Yes, the former poet laureate of the Greater Southwestern Scribes Society, which meets every third Thursday in the back of Sue's Salon in Cement, Texas, has done it again. (And remember, if you mention this column at Sue's Salon, you get a coupon for 7 percent off of her patented orange-mint hair removal paste. It really works, too. Sue's upper lip looks fantastic!)

As I'm sure you remember, the esteemed Fernie holds an associate's degree in postmodern comparative limerick studies from the University of Southern Panama's Correspondence College and has been featured five times in the *American Anthology of Poetry*. Just a few of his classics include "Oh, Staff Sergeant, My Staff Sergeant!," "Why Is the Man Always from Nantucket?," "The Squirrels Stopped Talking to Me

Today," and his latest, "Lenticular Haiku," which was the inside-cover poem in the most recent edition of the *Cement Area Greensheet*.

Sir Archie has decided of late that many of our old standards—proverbs, parables, fables, and the like—are in desperate need of updating to more accurately reflect our life and times today. So the Great One has blessed us with his latest work: "Words for the Now."

So without further ado, I give you Sir Archie Ferndoodle:

### "Words for the Now"
*by Archie Ferndoodle*

If at first you don't succeed,
Apply for a government bailout.

Slow and steady never goes viral.

One bad apple lands a reality television show.

Two wrongs make a nifty presidential debate.

Early to bed and early to rise requires Ambien and amphetamines.

A Rolling Stone gathers retirement benefits by now, surely.

Neither a borrower nor a lender be; now, regulatory agent,
that's where the safe money is.

This above all: of thine own self promote like crazy.

All that glitters isn't gold, but all that's gold can be sold 24 hours a day at
Achmed's Gold Emporium & Pawn.

A penny saved is a colossal waste of time.

What's good for the goose probably doesn't contain
enough artificial growth hormone.

A bird in the hand is worth a couple rounds of Avian Flu H5N1 vaccinations.

It's always darkest before the energy companies invest in their infrastructure.

A friend in need is everybody not in the "5 percent."

A man's home is his castle until it becomes the bank's castle.

Speak softly and carry a stun gun.

Practice makes perfect, but it still can't beat steroids.

Laughter is the best medicine unless you can afford real medicine.

Fool me once, shame on you. Fool me twice, and I'll sue your butt
for everything you've got, including mental distress and anguish.

Sticks and stones may break my bones, but defriending
me on Facebook? Now, that really hurts.

Actions speak louder than words, but rumors are even louder.

A stitch in time is not as easy as Velcro.

# HANDING OFF THE BALL AT MIDCOURT? SERIOUSLY?

Among my earliest memories of watching sporting events live and in person are yellowed images of a musty gymnasium with rickety wooden bleachers. You know, an old-world gym, built in the 1930s or '40s, with the rounded roof, many windows long painted shut, and those ghastly caged halide lights bright enough to cause welder's burn on your corneas. It was the mid-1960s, and I was a little kid, watching my oldest sister play junior high basketball. I'm not exactly sure how young I was, but I do remember that I was small enough to easily crawl under, in, and around all the tiny crevices in the bleachers to find hidden treasure—loose change, dropped candy, and the occasional dollar bill or two. It was a blast.

Early life lesson: Lollipops stuck to the floor are not good to eat.

What little I recall of the actual games was that, in those days, girls basketball differed radically from boys basketball. Girls' teams had to divide themselves into frontcourt and backcourt squads, and crossing the midcourt line was prohibited. It was the oddest thing, especially looking back now, to see a girl running full speed on a breakaway only to come to a screeching halt at midcourt to pass the ball off to her teammate. But no one really gave it a second thought then. To paraphrase Mr. Hornsby, that's just the way it was.

I have to tell you that growing up with two older sisters gave me enough insight to realize the ridiculous premise behind this Victorian-style rule. Conventional wisdom in those days was that the female constitution was much more delicate than that of the male of the species, so what competition our dainty girls were allowed to participate in was softened and slowed for their protection.

Horse patties.

A childhood spent variously trying to keep up with, fend off, outfight, outrace, outbite, outkick, run from, and savagely battle for bathroom rights against two merciless sisters taught me, often painfully, that girls are just as tenacious, spirited, and competitive as boys. Except their nails are longer.

It came as no surprise to me, then, when Billie Jean King beat the chauvinistic socks off of one Bobby Riggs in the "Battle of the Sexes" tennis match in 1973. Remember that? It was for $100,000, winner take all. (And one hundred grand was beaucoup money in '73.) Yes, Riggs was in his 50s, and sure, he hammed up the dominant male role to the hilt, and indeed, King was in her prime, but the action on the court spoke for itself. King blasted Riggs, 6-4, 6-3, 6-3, using the crafty old guy's defensive tactics against him. And if you thought Riggs tanked the match, think again. Not many people are aware that Riggs played another "Battle of the Sexes" match four months before the one against Riggs—and he defeated Margaret Court, one of the top women players of the time, 6-2, 6-1.

Not long after this was when Chris Evert and Martina Navratilova began their decades-long rivalry. As big a fan as I was of guys like Jimmy Connors and John McEnroe, I genuinely anticipated watching Chrissy and Martina go at it as much as any men's match. To my great surprise and delight, it was about this time, in the early 1980s, that I happened upon Navratilova in, of all places, the University of Texas at Arlington gym. She lived in the area at the time and worked out with the UTA women's basketball team to keep up her stamina. I was a UTA student, and I jogged in and around that old gym a lot. Martina walked by me once to get a drink of water, and there was not an ounce of fat on her body. She looked as if composed of granite. I blurted something about being a huge fan, and she smiled uneasily at me. Another crazed fan, great, I'm sure she was thinking.

Anyway, what got me thinking about how our society has long viewed women's sports—you know, with that second-class air of inferiority—were two recent developments. A phenomenon named Brittney and my youngest daughter, Jamie. If you were unaware, the Baylor University women's basketball team went 40-0 this year. Think about that. Forty wins, no losses. No college team—men's or women's—has ever done that. And anchoring that amazing team was one Brittney Griner, the six-foot-eight-inch dunking machine from Houston. Did you watch this team play? Lordy, I was more juiced to watch the women's playoffs than the men's this year. Incredible stuff. And it wasn't all Griner, either. When teams figured out how to shut her down (by double- and triple-teaming her), the Bears' outside shooters, such as Odyssey Sims, nailed them from long range.

And, oh, my daughter Jamie. It has been one of those dad things this year, I suppose, getting to watch my youngest run the half-mile. Sorry, they call it the 800 meters now. I was a trackster (Truman Administration, I believe) long ago, and it thrills me to watch a chip off the old block stride along that track. She asked me to run with her around the neighborhood, and after a couple of blocks of grunting and panting, I instructed Jay to go on ahead of me. Bad knee or something.

Handing off the ball at midcourt, indeed.

# WHERE'VE I BEEN, YOU ASK? DON'T ASK

Ahoy, fellow earthbound mugwumps. Your friendly psycho-neuro-spiritual travel agent is back. For those devoted few (OK, one) who follow Ye Olde Spouse week in and week out, please accept my hipdeep apologia for the extended absinthe. Absence. Whatever. For you occasional delvers into these parts, I've been gone, you see. Way. Far. Gone. And boy, are my arms tired (rimshot, applause).

Spouseman took some time off, seeking clarity, hoping for a gander at the real me and maybe even some face time with That That Is. None of that happened, so I cleaned up the paraphernalia and hauled the family down to Galveston. Then we took one of those giant floating cities on a cruise down Meh-hee-co way. I am still processing the whole thing.

If you've never been on one of these behemoth boats, imagine cramming the whole population of, say, Alpine or Marble Falls into a 12-story, 900-foot-long gently swaying apartment building with bad plumbing. Also imagine that each resident occupies living quarters approximately the size of an extra-wide Kenmore refrigerator box.

But there is cable TV. And little mints on your pillows. And every night, you find on your bed all your bathroom towels magically morphed into bizarre sea creatures, cute animals, or whatever else your cabin steward feels like crafting on a whim. I think our guy got bored or perhaps a bit miffed that I kept mispronouncing his name after the first couple of days because by the third night, we found our towels formed into a bust of Jeffrey Dahmer.

Now, your first day on board you must practice your lifesaving drill. Your lifesaving drill involves finding your way past dozens of stairs, bars, and cocktails in coconut shells to your assigned muster station, where you stand like a sweating dork with several hundred other sweating dorks, trying in vain to listen to the Filipino man in an inflatable life vest while, standing right next to you, three heavy-tonnage drunks from Odessa sing "It's Five O'Clock Somewhere" at the top of their lungs.

About all I was able to make out was the following:

"...very important to remember that unless you ..."

*"pour me somethin' tall an' strong!"*

"... must be inflated properly or ..."

*"make it a hurricane before I go insane!"*

"... could mean death by drowning. Have a wonderful cruise."

Although the pools aren't very big, there are a lot of them. There's a pool by the buffet, a pool by the giant-screen TV, a hot tub next to the casino, a pool on the Lido Deck, a water slide that ends in a pool on the Panorama Deck, etc. And next to each of these pools a heaving throng of scantily clad people jiggle endlessly to the Macarena. Yes, they're still playing that song. And no, the words "scantily," "clad," and "jiggle" shouldn't be misconstrued. The booties shaking here, wooh—let's just say this is bounty best left buried. Under many layers of opaque clothing, please. (shudder of remembrance here)

It's rather unfair of the cruise types, if you ask me, to have the buffet parked in such close proximity to the thundering, line-dancing herd. The blubbering booty renders the triple-cheese soup, skillet-seared steak, and warm chocolate melting cake a bit unsavory.

Everything you hear about the food is true, though. Good and bad. There's terrible fare, and there is some spectacular feasting to be had (chiefly at the sit-down dinners, mind you, where you're forced to dine every evening with the same blue hairs whose political views—slightly to the right of Hitler—are shared with you in excruciating detail at every sitting).

And yes, as the week wears on, your clothes will magically shrink. Just count on it.

The ports of call in the Western Caribbean jaunt are attractive enough, but you have just enough time in port to be accosted by an army of souvenir hawkers ("because you my friend, only $45 US"), buy a genuine Cozumel shot glass made in China, eat a meal authentic enough to send the mighty Montezuma himself running, and then crowd back onto the ship like so many sun-scorched cattle. Mooo. You gotta be back on board before nightfall, no exceptions.

It's all about the money, you see. And your smiling cruise ship people want your hard-earned hash to be slung on board, not on land. So you get a few hours off ship, max. And speaking of the green stuff, unless you are astronomically lucky, are a professional poker player from Amarillo, or are some kind of Rain Man, set not one foot in the ship's casino. Good God Almighty, you might as well just hand over a couple of C notes to the casino cashier and go to bed. I tried many games in there, and I'm here to tell you that cruise ship casino machines are tighter than Joan Rivers' face. You've been warned.

I hoped to meet some exotic people from far-away lands on our adventure. And I did. Our cabin steward, who fashioned a striking Ted Bundy towel bust our last night on board, was from Thailand, I think. Or maybe it was Seattle. But every single cotton-pickin' passenger I met was from Texas. It was like being in a Fort Worth bar every night, except with a pervasive septic aroma. OK, then, it was like being in a Lubbock bar every night. Period.

Oh, one more thing. Forget all that jazz about getting your sea legs. The rocking of the ship is not that bad; you get used to it. What's tough is getting your land legs back. I found myself at work the Monday after I got back, gently swaying and zig-zagging down the hall.

It took an hour and a half to convince my boss I wasn't off the wagon again.

# DISCOVERY OF 'DAD PARTICLE' A SIGNIFICANT SCIENTIFIC BREAKTHROUGH

Ponca City, Oklahoma (AP)—In a culmination of 50 years of theoretical speculation and weeks of intense media frenzy, two teams of researchers at the Fatherhood Institute for Research Nerds (FIRN) recently announced they had independently discovered evidence for the long-sought elementary particle that dictates behavior by dads and thus significantly impacts the family universe—the elemental unit popularly known as the "Dad Particle."

To thunderous applause from a standing-room-only crowd of domestic behaviorists, journalists, and several unknown men from the soup kitchen across the street gathered at FIRN—as well as from other groups of fatherhood researchers around the world watching by webcast—the leaders of the two teams said they had definitely observed a particle they termed a "Riggs bison," so named because this sub-atomic speck of matter found deep within the brains of fathers, interestingly enough, greatly resembles one-time tennis great Bobby Riggs riding an American bison.

"We have now found the missing cornerstone of fatherhood physics," said Rolf Molf, FIRN's director general. "We indeed have a discovery. We have observed a new particle common to all fathers. This astounding breakthrough will give wives, mothers, daughters, sons, and anyone else who might give a rat's behind some answers as to why fathers old and young do some of the amazingly dimwitted things they do. As to why this particle looks like Bobby Riggs riding a buffalo, we have no idea."

"Bison," interrupted Assistant Director General Haye Seed.

"Whatever," Molf said.

If there proves to be one and only one Riggs bison, its discovery would provide confirmation of the so-called Standard Model of Dad Behavior. "It appears to us that this 'Dad Particle' determines fundamental fatherhood characteristics, such as affinity for lying horizontal on couches during weekends, slipping an extra fiver to a grounded daughter, and watching reruns of old football games ad nauseum," said Molf. "On test subjects, we removed the Riggs buffalo and within days these men were shopping with their wives, asking directions from service stations, and actually limiting their beer intake to one or two cans on the weekend. It was remarkable."

"Bison," insisted Seed.

In 1964, two groups of dad theorists each proposed that the brain of the average American father is pervaded by a molasses-like field, now called the Riggs bison field. As fermions (father-like thoughts) pass through the field, they acquire mass. And a quite tasty molasses-like flavor, at that. Without this Riggs bison field, a dad's tendency to, say, hog the remote, would literally fall apart; even a father's boisterous belch would no longer exist.

One of the "fysicists," (shortened from "fatherhood physicists") Peter Short of the University of North Ponca City, predicted that if this field were hit by the right amount of estrogen energy, it would produce a unique phenomenon, which came to be known as the "knockdown dragout." Short was present at the FIRN announcement and said afterward: "For me, it is an incredible thing that has happened in my lifetime. Now, dads everywhere can point to this discovery and say, 'See? It's not my fault.'"

Discovery of the "Dad Particle" was made possible by the FIRN super collider, which took approximately an hour and a half to construct. Built atop the running track at Ponca City High School's Wildcat Stadium, the super collider sends two dads, mounted on tricycles, in opposite directions on the 400-meter track. When the dads collide, at super-slow speed, their heads are then immediately examined via MRI. The MRI results are then X-rayed, and the result is then mimeographed and faxed to the press box.

"It was there, in the Wildcat Stadium press box, where speculation first took hold that the Riggs buffalo may have been found," Molf said. "I still have goose bumps."

"Bison," Seed corrected.

# KETCHUP ON YOUR DOG? NOT IN CHICAGO. IT'S THE LAW. I THINK.

Salutations, my carefree cadre of cosmic cadets. Oh, mi amigos, sometimes the fates simply will not let you escape what you're trying to escape from because there's just no escape from the thing you wish to escape. From. Dig? I'll give you an e.g. Take the heat. Spouseman had a quasi-business trip to Chicago recently, so I folded the family into the Samsonites and jaunted off in earnest hopes of glorious non-triple-digit climes. Hah. The Big Guy doth chuckle. We stepped out of the cab from Midway Airport onto the baking intersection of Grand and Michigan and promptly melted into the pavement. Seems I packed the heat wave in with the family and the underwear. Thus I believe we lent a new meaning to the term "packing heat."

As we admired the downtown skyline, 29 cars, buses, and taxis immediately honked at us to get our Texas butts out of the road. Welcome to the City of Big Shoulders! There would be ample honking and sirens as the days progressed.

Actually, as the week went on the temps smoothed out a bit, and the constant Lake Michigan breeze felt downright nice. But Chi-town its own self was quite the learning experience.

Much of the Chicago scene involves eating. It's good eating, too, but there are rules. Statutes and laws even. For example, under no circumstances may anyone in the greater metropolitan city limits put ketchup or any squashed-tomato-like product on a hot dog. It is strictly verboten. Vendors display large signs to this effect. Onions, relish, mustard, pickles, peppers, paprika, parsley, sage, rosemary, thyme are all fine for your frankfurter, but no ketchup.

To wit, our stroll through Millennium Park near the hotel on our first day was jolted by the sight of two of Chicago's finest cuffing a man lying face-first in the grass. Uh oh, we thought. We'd been warned to be wary of big-city crime.

"What happened, officer?" I asked a backup policeman standing nearby.

"K.O.D.," the officer replied grimly.

"K.O.D.?"

"K.O.D. Ketchup On Dog. Stand back, please."

"I swear, I thought it was the mustard," the guy pleaded, his mouth and hands smeared a ghastly, guilty red. "It was a mistake!"

"Take him away."

Chicagoans take their dogs seriously. There's even a Wikipedia entry:

"A Chicago-style hot dog, or Chicago Dog, is a steamed or water-simmered all-beef frankfurter on a poppy seed bun. The dog is topped with yellow mustard; chopped white onions; bright green sweet pickle relish; a dill pickle spear; tomato slices or wedges; pickled peppers; and a dash of celery salt. The complete assembly of a Chicago hot dog is said to be 'dragged through the garden' due to the many toppings. Some variants exist, adding ingredients such as cucumber slices, but the canonical recipe *does not include ketchup*, and there is a widely shared, strong opinion among many Chicagoans and aficionados that ketchup is unacceptable. A number of Chicago hot dog vendors do not even offer ketchup as a condiment, while those who do often use it as a litmus test."

Or as part of a police sting, as the case may be.

There are plenty of culinary delights besides the eponymous dog, including some of the best Italian food west of New Jersey, but, again, there are attendant rules and regulations. Please pay attention, because although the folks we met in Chicago were friendly and affable, when it comes to food they mean business.

Near the famous Lincoln Park Zoo, for another e.g., there's a terrific pub/eatery called R.J. Grunt's. And at R.J. Grunt's, where the proprietors claim to have invented the modern-day salad bar, you can pile everything from aardvark shavings to zinnia petals on your scrumptious salad, but if you're caught sharing with a non-salad-bar patron—even your mom—you will be hauled off on an S.S.B.

We'd been in town for a few days by the time we hit Grunt's, so we were practically Chicagoans ourselves by this time. As they took away one particular crouton criminal, a wide-eyed tourist sidled up to me.

"What happened?" he asked.

"S.S.B."

"S.S.B.?"

"Sharing Salad Bar. Stand back, please."

But far and away our most exciting brush with Chicago's culinary commandments was at the one and only Billy Goat Tavern tucked under the bridge on Michigan Avenue. Yep, this is the place that inspired the classic Saturday Night Live "cheezeborger, cheezeborger, cheezeborger" skit.

It's all true. Except it's "no Pepsi, Coke" instead of the "no Coke, Pepsi" John Belushi recited in the SNL skit. Apparently, Belushi figured "no Coke, Pepsi" sounded funnier, and who can argue his comedic brilliance? All the rest you remember from the skit is right on, however. The waitress bullied us into not only "cheezeborgers" but double "cheezeborgers" at that—and they were worth it. I'm doing a Pavlovian salivation thing right now just typing about them.

And yes, there are no fries. No fries, cheeps. There's a great big sign warning you, so you've only yourself to blame if you get hauled away on an F.F.T.

"F.F.T.?"

"French Fry Try. Stand back, please."

# I FEEL FUNNY.
# AND NOT FUNNY HA HA.

Gentle readers, you must pardon me if this installment of my periodic, oft-nonsensical missives unto you appears somewhat professorial, pedantic, and/or prosodic. I must warn you from the start that in my ever-vigilant endeavors to explore the bounds of subject matter for this whimsical journalistic discourse—with precious little regard for my personal safety and body fat content, mind you—I sometimes cross the line between investigative reporting and life-endangering folly. Not unlike intrepid chroniclers before me, such as George Plimpton, Terry Southern, and Henry Cabot Henhouse III, I must at times insert my very own self into the dark heart of the topic at hand.

Therefore, be advised, then, that I am penning these words with the assistance and/or interference, as the case may be, of 200 milligrams of the analeptic monoamine-releaser modafinil. In other words, I'm all hopped up on a tab of prescription Provigil, the latest "wakefulness aid" to come down the off-label pike. And I must say at the outset that moment by moment, my intramuscular energy levels are increasing at an astonishing rate, while my cognitive abilities appear to be coalescing, dare I say multiplying, as I type. Note that I am also scrubbing the kitchen floor grout with a toothbrush, learning Mandarin Chinese via iPod, and performing a mental audit of our family's previous three years of Form 1040 Schedule A itemized deductions. Piece of cake, really.

Just as this generation of moms has discovered that dipping into their kids' Ritalin stash has rendered running the household a veritable breeze, folks who were recently prescribed Provigil tablets for narcolepsy or other sleeping disorders have found that a daily off-label popping of one of these minuscule motivators transforms them into super-functioning cerebretrons. Now, we had our own forms of Ritalin and Provigil back in the day. We called it speed. Except if you consumed enough of this heart-squeezing substance, say, to stay up all week during college finals, you could very well end up speeding right into the emergency room.

However, according to a recent ABC News segment on the growing crowd of Provigil partisans, this new wonder drug has no adverse side effects they can detect so far. Let me underline the so far. So far. There. I'll italicize it, also: *So far*. I mean, they've been studying this stuff how long, a year maybe? How tragic (or comic) would it be to witness a hefty portion of the population go running to their doctors claiming a sudden onset of narcolepsy so they can all hop on the Provigil Express only to gradually mutate into half-stallion, half-cyclops people in five years' time?

I don't know about you, but I'd rather not have many of my neighbors and friends become half-stallion, half-cyclops people. This isn't Arkansas.

The great dearth of longitudinal studies notwithstanding, Provigil sales have skyrocketed. Prescription sales have reportedly increased 73 percent in the last four years—to approximately $1.5 billion. That's billion. With a buh.

One guy, a Mr. Dave Asprey, who runs a billion-dollar (with a buh) Internet security firm, told ABC News he starts his day at about 4 in the a.m. Get this, Asprey once bounced out of bed, worked out for a couple of hours, flew 20 hours to Australia with no sleep, and then delivered a series of speeches that were so inspiring they were featured in the local newspapers.

How are we supposed to compete in the workplace with a Provigil Pete? I believe that employers should screen for Provigil in the same fashion athletes are checked for steroids or other performance-enhancing drugs. How on earth am I going to be able to justify my afternoon siesta when Pro-V Patty is in the next cubicle cross-referencing the company archives back to 1862? And what about all those Salesperson of the Month plaques that decorate your friendly car dealer's walls? I say if they discover that any of those top-sales guys were on Provigil that an asterisk must be placed by their names. The asterisk of shame.

Anyway, back to Mr. Asprey. As an experiment, ABC took the guy off the drug for several days, and he did admit he felt a bit "off." He even admitted his speech was altered! Hmm. Then he keeled over dead. OK, not really.

All I can report to you personally is that as I have been writing this column (and scrubbing the kitchen floor and learning Mandarin Chinese and self-auditing my tax returns back to 1933) I have experienced a certain mental expansion.

I also believe this is in large part due to the locus of the monoamine action of modafinil, which has also been the target of studies identifying effects on dopamine in the striatum and nucleus accumbens, as opposed to the noradrenaline in the hypothalamus and ventrolateral preoptic nucleus, as well as serotonin in the amygdala and frontal cortex. But you knew that. Duh.

Otherwise, I feel no adversefafctcts shatsoevr, infact I hav neveer flt btetr in... in ... hel p ... 9 ... 1.......1

# THERE'S FOOTBALL, AND THERE'S LIFE. BUT MAINLY THERE'S FOOTBALL.

It hit me the other day, my genteel tribe, as I sat watching the glorious first football weekend of the holy month of September. The remote—it hit me square in the back of the head. The wife trying to get my attention again; something about dinner or a burglar or something. That woman's got aim. Anyway, then it really hit me, as I listened to that specialized vocabulary that signals the start of a new season. That magical lexicon of the gridiron just so happens to have context—and in quite similar fashion, I might add—to the life of this middle-aged hubby, dad of two teenage girls (help me, Lord), owner of a thoroughly over-mortgaged house, and slumlord to two very ill-behaved pets (one fat, incontinent dog and one nasty, lethargic cat).

I began listing in my head these terms that carry dual meaning in my quaint little life, but the terms kept slipping out of my head where the wife konked me with the remote. The den started getting cluttered with all these words falling to my feet, so I figured I should sweep them up and list them.

So here they are, expressions o' the gridiron and their "other" meanings, in alphabetical order for your convenient reference:

**All-out Blitz.** Usually run when Mom's away, this is a designed play in which both daughters beseech Dad in unison to pleeeeeease take them to the corner store for basic life necessities (e.g., gum, ice cream, Pringles).

**End Around.** Another regular from the daughter playbook, this is a misdirection play used to call Mom's or Dad's attention to one daughter while the other one either (A) sneaks in or out of the house; (B) cleans up whatever she broke; or (C) dashes to the bathroom to attempt repairs to her purple hair dye job.

**False Start.** Called almost exclusively on Mom, this mix-up occurs whenever the family is set to go out, either to a restaurant, shopping, movie, etc., and Mom says "I'm ready." Family members then wait in the car for another 25 minutes before realizing that "I'm ready" means "another half-hour" with regard to Mom.

**Illegal Shift.** This penalty is called on either one daughter or the other, depending on who stole the front passenger position in the car after the first daughter clearly called "shotgun" before the outing began.

**Nickel Back.** This term refers to the change Dad often gets back from mall excursions by Daughter #1, Daughter #2, or Mom—or, more often, all three of them running the same play. (See also End Around.)

**Pass Interference.** A tactic used almost exclusively by Dad, this is a time-honored anti-flirting measure employed by dads all over, usually achieved by physically stepping in between the line of sight of boys and young men trying to catch the eye of Daughter #1 or vice-versa. Recently, much to Dad's dismay, this has begun to apply to Daughter #2, as well. (See also Shotgun Formation.)

**Pooch Kick.** Often inadvertent (but sometimes not), this clumsy play occurs when Ralph the dachshund gets underfoot waiting for scraps in the kitchen. Penalty depends on distance pooch is kicked.

**Prevent Defense.** This is a tactic often utilized by Dad to avoid manual labor, mostly on weekends, by pretending to be soundly asleep on the couch (or whatever furniture he happens to be lounging on) when called upon by Mom.

**Shotgun Formation.** Although an actual shotgun is optional here, this is the classic formation used by Dad by sitting on the front-porch swing when daughters are due home from dates.

**Touchback.** A nerve-wracking phenomenon occurring almost exclusively on family road trips, this is when daughters #1 and #2 vie for territorial rights in the back seat of the car. The constantly recurring touchback commotion almost inevitably ends with the command, "If I have to turn this car around!"

**Two-minute Warning.** This mad scramble by Dad is triggered by the appearance of the mother-in-law's car in front of the house. It takes mom-in-law approximately two minutes to make it from her car to the house, by which time Dad must have himself hidden away in the den or the master bedroom. If not, he is often subjected to many **Bombs** and **Cheap Shots** regarding personal appearance, yard maintenance, career ambition, etc.

# HERE'S TO THE OLYMPIC MOTTO: SWIFTER, HIGHER, STRONGER, SNEAKIER

Ah, my cantankerous cohort, if you're like me, you've been basking in all the reflected, tape-delayed glory of the London Olympics, no? And if you're like me, me, you've been inspired by the relentless spirit and determination of Olympians such as South African sprinter Oscar Pistorius, who runs on specially made prosthetic springs. Yes? And if you're like me, you've been absolutely flabbergasted by that water polo player from Belarus who was born with only a head. No? OK, wait a minute.

Seriously, in what has otherwise been a stultifying, sweltering summer, the XXXth Olympiad from jolly old England has supplied a refreshing sports fix. Maybe I shouldn't use the word "fix." Because, alas, as with just about every other one of these world block parties, there has been juicy controversy. For example, did you catch the bantamweight boxing match where the Japanese guy knocked down his opponent six times—*and lost*? I'm not one to yell collusion in a crowded auditorium, but you be the judge. The referee for the match, Turkmenistan's Ishanguly Meretnyyazov, ruled that Azerbaijan's Magomed Abdulhamidov defeated Satoshi Shimizu, even though Abdulhamidov could scarcely stand up for the decision. Shimuzi was running around doing backflips. Sanity eventually settled in and the decision was overturned—and referee Meretnyyazov was booted out of the Olympics.

Meretnyyazov later admitted to being in cahoots with Abdulhamidov, apparently due to Turkmenistan's longstanding desire to build a Wal-Mart on land owned by Abdulhamidov's uncle, Spraodovlugyzatsonivyplakolov Urryupanpayemov.

But that wasn't even the major hullabaloo. Four, count 'em, four women's doubles teams were disqualified from the badminton competition for intentionally losing matches to gain a more favorable draw in the next round. Heavens to Murgatroyd! The BWF was shocked, shocked, I say. (That's the Badminton World Federation to you and me—and yes, there is such a thing.) Let's back up a minute here. I can see both sides. This is the Olympics, and fans paid plenty of precious pounds to see their favorite shuttlecock swatters play their very best. But. And it's a big but. In many other sports, easing up on the gas and resting yourself when you've been assured a spot in the next round is done all the time. Look at the NFL (if you can). When a team has clinched a playoff spot, the coach often decides to rest his starters—and the team often loses a meaningless next game.

Both sides have a point, but there is a much bigger picture to consider. And that much bigger picture is this: Badminton? Seriously? Don't get me wrong; I'm a staunch believer in anything that gets one off the couch and moving about. Yes, I am an athletic supporter. I'm just not so sure about awarding Olympic medals to folks who compete in what is essentially a backyard pastime while waiting for the burgers. I mean, criminy, we might as well have Olympic horseshoes or Olympic barbecueing. Hmmm. Come to think of it, Olympic barbecueing might be fun—until controversy rears its ugly head again. "U.S. Olympic Barebecueist Lee Roy Heinz was disqualified today when his charcoal tested positive for lighter fluid."

Well, get this. Olympic barbecueing sounds positively mainstream compared to some other events that actually saw the light of day in Olympic games past. For example, solo synchronized swimming was a real Olympic event from 1984 to 1992. Think about that for a minute: Solo. Synchronized. Swimming. Other former events include tug of war, rope-climbing, and, of course, the plunge for distance. What was the plunge for distance, you ask? In this spine-tingling event, competitors dived into a pool and were required to remain motionless underwater for one minute or until their heads broke the surface. The plunger who recorded the longest distance won.

"Grandpa, how did you win your Olympic medal again?"

"I was a world-class plunger."

This event, of course, gave rise to the short-lived Olympic Marco Polo competition.

Here's another one: the one-handed weight lift. I'm serious. Each competitor had to perform lifts with each hand, with the winner determined from the combined score. Although this event was discontinued after only three Olympic games, it did lead to the one-handed pole vault, one-armed rowing competition, and one-legged mile run. The one-legged mile was held only once, however. Competitors had yet to finish two weeks after the closing ceremonies. Ah, well. See you in Rio.

# ROCKY MOUNTAIN HIGH, IN...UH...WOAH, WHAT?

So I'm sitting, slightly askew, on the couch the other evening, wincing through the throbs of a pulled lower back, trying ever so hard to catch glimpses of "60 Minutes" in between intermittent stabs of electric pain. Note to self: It takes two people to move the wife's giant potted sago palm.

Lo, mi amigos, there on my favorite TV news magazine was an investigative piece on the burgeoning business built on the manufacture and sale of, shall we say, pungent herbs in states such as Colorado and California. For medicinal purposes only, mind you. According to Steve Kroft and crew, 17 states have now legalized the medical use of (cannabis...shhh) for treatment of ailments such as glaucoma, side effects of chemotherapy, nausea, and, aha, chronic pain. There are, get this, more than 200 medical marijuana (there, I said it) dispensaries in Denver alone! That means there are more corner Grass-n-Go markets than there are Starbucks in the Mile High City.

Talk about a budding industry. Rimshot. Applause, applause.

It's interesting to note that although an air of legitimacy is lent to this state-sanctioned drugstore doobage—with barcodes on individual plants and white-coated THC technicians advising patients on characteristics and properties of each strain—that vestiges of the headshop hippie days still linger, specifically with the nicknames attached to different types of product. Some samples: Jack Frost, Blue Dream, Purple Haze, Skywalker Special, Accidental Tourist, Gracie Slick, Agent Orange—and yep, there is still Acapulco Gold.

Try as I might, I'm having a bit of difficulty envisioning an elderly glaucoma sufferer, say, an 85-year-old grandmother with a walker, toddling into her corner Hash-n-Dash. But here goes:

Eighty-five-year-old Grandmother With Walker: "Hello, Doctor Stoner."

White-coated THC Technician: "Please, Mrs. Baker, I'm not a doctor, just a technician. Call me Moon Skye. How's the glaucoma this week?"

Eighty-five-year-old Grandmother With Walker: "Not good, Dr. Moonpie. I ran out of the Lemon Skunkweed two days ago and couldn't get in until today."

White-coated THC Technician: "Tell you what. We're out of Lemon right now, but we're having a special on Night Train Nebula."

Eighty-five-year-old Grandmother yadda: "Oh, that Night Train makes me paranoid. Do you have any Blue Monkey Balls?"

White-coated THC blah etc.: "Sorry, Mrs. Baker."

Eighty-yadda so on: "Oh, all right. Half-ounce Night Train then. And do you have any papers?"

White blah etc.: "Sure thing, Mrs. B."

Eightyzzzz: "Groovy."

Sounds hokey, yes, but this is big, big biz. As in the billions of dollars. It's a green industry in more ways than one. And for those nonsmokers looking for relief, these pot practitioners make cannabis-infused cookies, candy, ice cream, sports drinks, pills, olive oil—you name it. If it can be ingested, it can be toasted.

Yet, as I squirm here on my couch, twinging with what feels like lower back labor pains, I must settle for a measly couple of ibuprofen, seeing as how Texas doesn't square with Colorado's views on pain-relieving plants and such. I know we're the big, fat belt buckle of the Bible sash and all, but if cooler heads prevailed in the Legislature (get it? heads), we'd see the obvious benefits—namely, crazy stacks of Benjamins in state coffers. And don't quote me on this, but I bet we'd see a reduction in violent crime and speeding offenses. In fact, I'd predict a spike in tickets and warnings issued for driving *too far under* the speed limit. And I imagine there'd be a quantum leap in late-night sales of Doritos and caramel corn.

Texas being Texas, of course, we could put our own brand on the business. The possibilities would be practically endless: Texas Tea, Lone Star Lids, Dallas Dimebag, Galveston Ganja, Houston Homegrown, Beaumont Buds…you get the idea.

Naah. I don't see it happening. That sort of thing is viewed as just too dangerous here in the big state. Besides, there'd be no room for dispensaries amid the gun shops and liquor stores.

# FIN